The Life and Loves of Karen Romano

RAYNETTE MITCHELL

Mitchell Media

Copyright © 2020, Revised 2024, by Raynette Mitchell

All rights reserved. The moral right of the author has been asserted.

No part of this publication may be reproduced, distributed, or transmitted in any form or by any means, electronic or mechanical, including photocopying, recording, scanning, or by an information storage and retrieval system, without the prior written permission of the publisher. For permission requests, contact Mitchell Media at jetoboy@bigpond.com.

The story, all names, characters, and incidents portrayed in this production are fictitious. No identification with actual persons (living or deceased), is intended or should be inferred.

Cataloguing in Publication entry is available from the National Library of Australia – http://catalogue.nla.gov.au

Raynette Mitchell/The Life and Loves of Karen Romano

Paperback ISBN 978-0-6488426-4-4

eBook ISBN 978-0-6488426-5-1

Second Edition, 2024

CONTENTS

1. MEETING JOHN	1
2. LOVING JOHN	17
3. LOSING JOHN	24
4. MEETING MARTIN	32
5. UNDERSTANDING MARTIN	36
6. AN EXCITING NEW VENTURE	61
7. TRUE FRIENDS	70
8. A MOVE TO THE COUNTRY	83
9. A NEW HOBBY?	96
10. PAUL'S STORY—Part One	108
11. PAUL'S STORY—Part Two	136
12. THE AFFAIR	151
13. SURPRISE, SURPRISE!	173
14. THE DINNER	185
15. A DAGGER TO THE HEART	199
16. SOCIETY'S RULES	204
17. AND SO IT GOES...	208
AUTHOR'S NOTES	211
ACKNOWLEDGEMENTS	212
AUTHOR BIO	215
AND COMING UP NEXT...	217

"How complicated and unpredictable the machinery of life really is."

– Kurt Vonnegut Jr.

1

MEETING JOHN

1978

Karen Romano led a pretty dull life. The most exciting thing she had done in her eighteen years so far was to secure a job in a solicitor's office in the city—which says it all—clerk in a law office! Life for an eighteen-year-old doesn't get much more boring.

Until the day she met John Pascoe, when things began to get interesting.

It happened on a Saturday morning as Karen trawled through the magazine section of the local newsagent's, trying to decide which home magazine to buy for her mother. Unfortunately, there wasn't much to choose from. From the corner of her eye, she spied what looked like the last copy of *Home Beautiful* and reached for it, only to come away empty-handed when the young man standing next to her picked it up before she could. He turned and smiled a 1000-watt smile at her and said: 'Your need seems to be greater than mine,' and gallantly handed the magazine to her as he inclined his head and made a mock bow.

She hesitated for a moment, on the brink of saying, 'No, you take it,' but before she had a chance to speak, he said, 'It's my mother's favourite magazine, but I'd happily let you have it if you'll have a coffee with me to compensate.'

Karen smiled gratefully as he handed the magazine to her and, emboldened by his approach, replied, 'that's kind of you. A coffee would be great.'

He extended his hand and said, 'I'm John Pascoe, by the way.'

'How do you do, John Pascoe. I'm Karen Romano.' Karen smiled inwardly as she tried to conceal her shyness with a formal reply. Not used to this type of situation, she felt awkward and gauche—and she hoped it didn't show.

They found a table in the corner of the cafe next door and settled down to chat. It wasn't long before Karen stretched out her legs under the table and began to relax, and when John asked her whether she was studying or if she worked, she replied, 'Both, actually. I'm working at a law firm in the city and studying to become a paralegal. How about you, John? What do you do?' *Ask people about themselves,* her mother had always said. *Try not to dwell on yourself too much.*

'What a coincidence. I'm in my third year of law at Sydney Uni. Wow, imagine if we got together, we'd be a force to be reckoned with!' And they both laughed.

They talked and laughed for the next couple of hours, drinking coffee and enjoying each other's company. Karen even agreed to a second cup, although she never had more than one cup of coffee a day. By then, she didn't care if she had the shakes for the rest of the day; it was worth it. Finally, John picked up his car keys, pushed his chair back from the table, and stood.

'I really must go. I have to pick my mum up from the station soon.' He paused momentarily and raised one eyebrow as he added, 'How about we do this again?'

Karen had enjoyed the past couple of hours more than she thought she would. This guy was so easy to talk to, and that smile!

'That would be lovely, John. How about the same place, same time next week?'

She couldn't believe she'd said that and felt the blood rush to her cheeks as embarrassment engulfed her, but John laughed. 'Great, see you then.'

Karen looked forward to seeing him again the following Saturday morning and hoped he hadn't forgotten. When she arrived at the cafe at the arranged time, there he was, sitting at the same table, reading the paper. He looked up and beamed that beautiful smile at her as she walked over to the table and sat.

'Hello, it's great to see you again,' he said, standing as she settled into her chair.

'Hi. It's good to see you too, John.' She smoothed her new floral skirt, bought especially for this occasion, over her knees and pushed her long blonde hair back off her face as their coffee arrived. He'd ordered before she'd even arrived. *Such confidence!* She thought enviously.

Now when she saw him again, he was not quite as she remembered. His hair was blonder than she thought, and she was sure it was longer—he must have had it cut. Although not particularly handsome, John had a pleasant, open face and a smile that could light up a room. His self-confidence twinkled in his blue eyes. He was wearing chinos and a polo shirt today, very Ivy League. Overall, John made quite an impression.

Once again, they chatted easily and comfortably and time passed unnoticed. As they were preparing to leave, John suggested they exchange phone numbers.

'Good idea,' Karen replied, as she fished around in her handbag for a pencil and paper.

As John stood and pushed his chair in, he casually asked, 'Would you like to go out for dinner one night? A new place has opened in Surry Hills that sounds good. Do you like Thai?'

'I love Thai. And I'd love to go.' Karen suddenly felt warm. She knew she was grinning like an idiot, but she couldn't help it. 'When did you have in mind?'

'How about Friday night? We could celebrate the end of the working week!'

Friday night's dinner was the start of many more dinners, and lunches, and movies. What began as a warm friendship developed into deep affection. Karen became infatuated with John as they gradually got to know each other, and she had a strong feeling he felt the same. He was so easy to be with—cheeky, charming, and respectful. She loved that he remembered birthdays and their anniversary, the way he lightly touched her shoulder whenever he walked behind her chair.

Somewhere, sometime, during those heady early days, John introduced Karen to sex. She didn't enjoy it at first, she couldn't relax and let herself go. But Karen wasn't the first chaste, innocent girl John had dated, and his experience eventually put her at ease. She soon responded to his patient, loving ways, and their sex life became something she enjoyed almost as much as he did.

A few months later, Karen, who lived at home with her mum and dad, summoned up the courage and asked them if she could invite John over for dinner to meet them.

'Of course,' replied her mum, Evelyn, with genuine delight. 'We would love to meet John. Can you find out what he likes and if he's allergic to anything? It would be terrible to serve the wrong thing.'

Karen smiled inwardly as she wrapped her arms around her mum in a warm hug. It would be an important occasion for her mother, who loved to cook, as they rarely entertained.

She was concerned John might find her parents a bit prim and proper. Her mother was Australian, her father—Italian born—was a naturalised Australian. Their house, although neat and tidy, was an average post-war brick bungalow in an average suburb.

During the afternoon of the big night, the two women set and decorated the table: the best tablecloth, linen napkins, and the family silver, which were only used on special occasions, were brought out. The candles Karen had given her mother the previous Christmas sat in the centre of the table; the crystal glassware sparkled. Pleased with their handiwork, the two women looked at each other and beamed.

Shortly before John was due to arrive, Karen suggested she and her mother have a little chat with her dad. Karen adored her father, but he could be volatile—a typical Italian 'papa'. A few words before the event might stave off any embarrassing moments.

'Frank,' Evelyn called. 'Frank. Could you come inside for a minute?'

Frank was busy in the back garden tending his precious grape vines. He'd showered and changed into the clothes Evelyn had laid out for him and was ready for the evening, but he still couldn't resist wandering around the vines with the pruning shears at the ready. He reluctantly put down the shears and removed his gardening gloves before coming inside to where the two women were sitting. Both looked up and smiled as he sat down.

'Now Frank,' Evelyn began, her hands clasped together as if she was about to break into song.

'Now Dad,' Karen reiterated, her arms folded over her chest in an attempt to look serious and intimidating.

Both women started giggling, but Evelyn turned serious and said, in her most endearing voice, 'Now Frank, tonight is important. We're meeting John for the first time and it would be good if you could be careful of what you say and do. Please don't start telling rude jokes. And don't talk politics—you know your opinions don't always match other people's. The last thing we need is for you to get on your soapbox and start in on the Government. And for God's sake, don't have so much to drink you start speaking Italian.' At this point, both women burst out laughing.

Karen hugged her father and kissed his cheek. 'Can I trust you to be a good boy?' she asked, laughing and frowning at the same time.

Her father, mock-outraged, made imaginary notes on the palm of his hand, muttering, 'Don't do this, don't do that, don't do the other.' He grinned at Karen and said, 'What if you end up marrying this guy? I'll have to keep that up for the rest of my life!' But he knew this boyfriend was somehow special and promised to be on his best behaviour.

The evening went well. Mrs. Romano served a delicious meal and Karen's father was a great raconteur who told entertaining stories, some moving, some hilarious. Karen could tell John was comfortable and relaxed and the evening could not have been any more enjoyable.

Until Mr. Romano brought out his home-made grappa.

As is traditionally Italian, Frank Romano had been growing his own grapes and making his own wine ever since he and Evelyn bought their own place. The reason they had decided on this house was because of the large backyard; plenty of room to put down grape vines. He'd been harvesting them every year and had honed his wine-making skills to an almost professional level. Last year's red had been particularly fine. Even Luigi, who lived two doors up, had been impressed, and he was almost impossible to please. But the grappa was his pride and joy, his bright shining star in a midnight sky of faintly twinkling reds and whites.

'This is the best grappa I've ever made. You are going to love it,' Frank said, as he proudly poured the syrupy liquid into two ruby coloured, gold embossed, Venetian liqueur glasses.

'This year, I built a special trellis for the vines. Best thing I ever did,' Frank explained, as he stood holding the two drinks as if he was loathe to part with one of them. 'The vines love it. This grappa is the finest and clearest so far.'

Oh no, thought Karen, *he's up and running on his favourite subject.*

He handed John the small liqueur glass containing the clear liquid.

John drank the nip down in one mouthful.

Karen had only ever had one nip of her father's grappa, but it was enough to know she would never have another—it was like drinking dynamite, only worse!

Poor John, Karen thought. *I know what he's going through right now. He's probably thinking he's going to die, that his heart is going to stop any minute. Probably can't talk or even see clearly. And now Dad was insisting he have another 'nip' because the grappa got better the more you drank!!*

In alarm, Karen grabbed her father's arm and squeezed it as she blurted out, 'Dad! No more. Can't you see his eyes are glazing over? Your grappa is deadly.'

Frank took a step back as John crashed down onto the sofa, legs akimbo, coughing uncontrollably. Karen rushed to his side and, grabbing a magazine from the coffee table, began fanning his face and rubbing his back with her hand. As the coughing subsided, she called out to her mother: 'Mum, quickly. Coffee, and make it strong.'

Even half an hour and 2 cups of Mrs. Romano's espresso coffee later, there was no way Karen was going to let John drive home. She insisted on getting a taxi for him. By the time the cab arrived, John was able to stand unassisted and could speak coherently. He thanked Mr. and Mrs. Romano profusely for a wonderful evening before Karen walked him out to the taxi and helped him into the back seat. He had trouble with his seat belt and as Karen leaned in to help him with it, he kissed her cheek and whispered in her ear, 'I love you, Karen.'

Flustered, she stepped back from the vehicle and closed the door.

Her heart sang as she stood there in the driveway and watched the car disappear into the night, even as she admitted to herself it was probably the grappa talking.

Karen's lips slowly turned up at the corners as she sat on the sunny side of the train on the way to work the following morning. She chuckled to herself as she remembered the events of the previous night. Poor John. She should have warned him about the grappa. Even so, she couldn't help grinning every time the image of him—eyes bulging, struggling to breathe, unable to speak after downing the grappa in one mouthful—crossed her mind. Although all that coughing wasn't good.

As the train rattled along and she basked in the morning sunlight that eked its way through the grimy train window, his last words to her as she helped him with the seat belt repeated over and over in her head. *I love you. I love you. I love you.* She knew it was because of the grappa, but it made her feel warm and fuzzy to recall the words.

On Wednesday of the following week they met for a drink after work and as he placed their glasses of white wine on the small table in the corner—the table which had become their favourite place in the wine bar—John said, 'Just wondering if you'd like to come to my parents' place for dinner one night soon. They'd love to meet you.'

'I'd love to,' replied Karen, carefully toning down her excitement at the thought of meeting 'the parents'. John was an only child, and she knew he was close to his mum and dad. It would be interesting to watch their interactions.

By Karen's standards, it was a big deal to meet your boyfriend's parents, and she wanted to make a good impression. Her mother suggested she wear a pair of tailored slacks and a silk blouse with the beautiful velvet flats and cashmere cardigan she and Frank had given her for her birthday. Although it wasn't Karen's choice—she would have preferred the new black minidress with shoestring straps and the five-inch heels she'd recently bought—her mum was in John's parents' age bracket and it would probably be a better idea to go with her suggestion.

The big night arrived. She wore her fair hair loose on her shoulders and her makeup was discreet, although Karen would have liked more eyeliner and mascara to go with the paler pink lipstick. The colours of the blouse and slacks went well together, and the dove-grey cardigan complimented her eyes. And she smelled delicious! A quick spray of Arpege perfume on her throat completed the right image. Karen twirled in front of the hall mirror, pleased with the reflection shining back at her, as she listened for the sound of John's car in the drive.

In the early days of their relationship, they talked briefly about where they lived. John told her he lived in a flat downstairs at the back of his parents' house—he couldn't afford to move away from home completely while he was still at Uni, so the flat was a compromise until he graduated. Karen was envious. Although she still lived at home with her mum and dad, she wanted to move out and become independent as soon as she could afford it.

These things crossed her mind as they turned into his street.

Mmmm, nice area, she thought. *I can see the bay from here.*

But she was taken aback when they pulled into the drive of a magnificent white two-story house of grand proportions set among exquisitely manicured gardens and lawns. A sandstone terrace, which ran the full width of the house, softened what could have been a stark, contemporary exterior, and the antique lanterns framing the front entrance gave the house a warm and welcoming appeal.

The front door opened as they walked up the steps, and Mrs. Pascoe ushered them into an exquisite marble-floored foyer. Karen couldn't help glancing up at the magnificent crystal chandelier which hung from the five-metre-high ceiling. A wide curved staircase with fancy black wrought-iron balustrading disappeared into the floor above.

John's mother was taller than Karen had imagined and wore her mid-brown hair in a short, straight bob. Her red-painted nails stood out against the pale skin of her slender long-fingered hands, but her rather formal high-necked dark green frock and matching mid-heeled shoes gave her a slightly schoolmarmish appearance.

John introduced them.

'I'm very pleased to meet you, Karen,' said Mrs. Pascoe as John introduced them. 'We've heard a lot about you. You've made quite an impression on John.'

As Mr. Pascoe walked up the hall toward them, John said, 'And this is my father. Dad, this is Karen.'

It was obvious where John got his irresistible smile from when Mr. Pascoe smiled and extended his hand. 'Well, hello, Karen,' he said, beaming, as they shook hands. 'I'm so pleased to meet you. Please, call us Judy and Ron.'

'It's a pleasure to meet you both—Judy and Ron,' Karen said, smiling broadly as she acknowledged each of them.

So far, so good, thought Karen. *Wow, this is some house*!

Ron led them into the sunroom which overlooked the bay. He poured drinks for them and the four chatted amiably. The sunset from this room was breathtaking. Although they were facing almost east, the fiery red setting sun was reflected in the clouds in the eastern sky, giving the area an ethereal pink hue.

I guess this is a waterfront block. Twinkling lights outside caught Karen's eye, and she turned her head to look out the picture window and down into the back area behind the house. Tiny flickering lights wound around the trunk of a large Jacaranda tree in the centre of the lawn. *What a lovely back garden*, Karen thought, as she sipped her drink and made small talk with Ron and Judy.

Ron was about to top up their drinks when John stood and said, with a wink in Karen's direction, 'Karen, come downstairs and I'll show you where I live,' and he took her hand and led her down a short flight of stairs which opened out into a large, airy room overlooking the back garden.

Karen suppressed a gasp as she took in the room. It wasn't just the expensive furnishings, but the quiet, warm ambience that wrapped itself around her. She stood very still, looking around, her eyes dancing from one beautiful piece to another.

Several magnificent oriental rugs were casually scattered about on the walnut-coloured timber floor. An old, comfortable-looking tan leather lounge and a slightly younger wing-backed armchair and matching ottoman sat opposite each other, looking as if they had been there for centuries. One wall consisted of floor-to-ceiling bookcases, some sections of which featured glass doors to protect what Karen supposed were law books. French doors led out to a long, narrow terrace, which then led onto the lawn. Against the opposite wall stood a walnut antique leather-topped Queen Anne desk on which sat a green banker's lamp and a scattering of papers and textbooks. A modern ergonomic black leather office chair sat snugly under the desk, which appeared incongruous against the mellow old furniture and oriental rugs. The whole thing reeked of money.

'What a beautiful room,' exclaimed Karen. 'It must be gorgeous in the mornings.'

'It is a lovely room. Used to be the dead area under the house until Mum had it built in for me before I started Uni. Sunrise from this room is spectacular. Allow me to show you the bedroom,' he said with another wink, and they giggled as he led the way.

The bedroom led off the apartment's living room. It was another well-proportioned room with French doors leading onto the same terrace. The timber floor flowed through from the main room and was bare except for an animal-skin rug between the bed and the French doors. The large bed stood against the back wall, and a majestic map of the world, as wide as the bed, hung above. A menacing and mysterious sound system, something that was beyond Karen's comprehension, stood like a sentry on the opposite wall. A door led into a tiny, all-white bathroom with chrome accessories and navy towels.

'What a fabulous setup you've got here. It must be very conducive to studying in such lovely surroundings, and so quiet.'

'It is. I go upstairs for meals or if I want to watch TV. Mum would like me to spend more time with them upstairs, but most nights, I'd rather be down here where I can be on my own, play my music, and study. I should finish Uni next year, and I'll be free as a bird then.' A pause, and then: 'I guess we'd better go back upstairs and let Dad make us another drink before dinner or they'll be wondering what we're up to down here.' He laughed that charming laugh as he took her hand and they walked back upstairs.

Karen wondered what he meant by 'I'll be free as a bird,' and 'Mum would like me to spend more time with them.' She filed that away in the back of her mind for future reference.

Dinner was superb, Judy was a gourmet cook. The Moroccan Chicken was perfect, the piquant North African spices counterbalanced by the cinnamon and dates, served with apricot rice—a meal to remember. The sweets looked wonderful—a crystal bowl of what appeared to be a type of layered trifle. When Karen took her first bite, she was surprised at how the rich citrus flavour combined beautifully with the chocolate curls that decorated the whole thing.

'I've never tasted this before. It is divine. What is it?' Karen asked, not caring if she appeared ignorant or naïve.

'It's called Orange Blossom Delizia,' replied Judy, with a smile that reminded Karen of the Cheshire cat in Alice in Wonderland. 'Not easy to make but well worth the effort, don't you think?'

'The entire meal was fabulous, thank you, Judy.' Karen meant every word.

'Do you cook, Karen?'

'Not really,' she replied as she folded her napkin neatly and placed it on the table. 'I live at home with my mum and dad, so I don't get much of an opportunity to cook. Not that I want to; I really don't enjoy it much. I don't think I'll ever be much of a cook.'

When they had finished dinner, Ron suggested they move to the lounge for coffee, but first, Karen helped Judy clear the table, carrying plates and dishes into the kitchen. As she placed some plates on the countertop, Judy glanced sideways at her and said, in a certain tone, not unlike one used by imperious school principals, 'You know, if you've got any ideas of a future with John, you'd better learn to cook. He's used to good food.'

The hairs on the back of Karen's neck stood up, and she felt a chill run up her spine.

'It was a lovely night, thank you, John,' Karen said in the car as John drove her home. 'Your parents are nice. Your mother is a superb cook.'

'They thought you were lovely, too.'

Karen smiled to herself and thought, *But I'm glad it's over.*

2

LOVING JOHN

John was good looking, charming, and with wealthy parents, how could she not fall in love with him? He was her first love. She had been out with several guys before but had tired of them quickly, whereas John was so interesting, so entertaining, so easy to love.

Although he had never actually said 'I love you,' aside from that one time when he was drunk on grappa, Karen was sure he did—his thoughtfulness, his consideration of her feelings, his touch, their lovemaking, his deference to her parents. And she knew she loved him. For the first time in her life, she knew what it felt like to be in love. It wasn't something she had thought much about in the past, but now it had happened to her, she could barely think about anything else. She felt happier than she had ever felt before. Even her eyes were more sparkly, her hair looked healthy and shiny, and she felt like she was smiling at everyone!

Over a glass of wine at the Wine Bar after work one evening, John placed his hand over Karen's and looked very hard at her. 'I've been thinking.'

She was immediately all ears. Whenever John said ' I've been thinking,' it was usually followed by, 'Why don't we . . .?'

'I've been thinking,' he said again. 'We get on so well, and we have such a good time when we're together, why don't we move in together?'

Karen was dumbfounded, momentarily speechless as her hand involuntarily covered her mouth in case she squealed out loud. She was elated at the idea, and the fact John had been thinking about it. Moving in together hadn't occurred to her before this moment. She beamed at him. 'I think that's the best idea you've ever had, and you've had some good ones. Let's drink to that.' And they ordered a bottle of champagne.

Karen's mind was overflowing with images of what it would be like to live in John's gorgeous apartment at the back of his parents' house. The beautiful living room and bedroom, both overlooking the lawn down to the water. She pictured the two of them sitting on the jetty on a warm weekend morning, drinking coffee, soaking up the sun, reading the Sunday papers.

Hmm, I hope we can do something about adding a little kitchenette to the flat so we can be completely self-contained and not have to eat upstairs all the time.

As she sipped her champagne, Karen decided now was as good a time to talk about it.

But when she did, John took both of her hands in his and looked into her eyes. 'There is no way we are going to live in my flat, not with my mother living above us, trying to control our lives every minute of every day. No way!'

Wow, where did that come from? Karen had never known John to be so forceful, so definite about anything before.

'We'll find somewhere, well away from my parents, and yours. I love Mum and Dad, as I'm sure you love your mother and father, but we don't want to start our lives together living under their influence.'

'Agreed,' Karen said, and clinked her glass with John's. So, her feelings of apprehension about John's mother were correct. The hairs on the back of Karen's neck were never wrong.

Days later, when John told his parents he and Karen were moving in together, his father looked pleased, but a strange look passed across his mother's face, a look of disdain, of disapproval. She quickly recovered and smiled, almost genuinely, 'Oh, that's lovely, dear. I'll arrange to have a kitchenette added to your apartment. I'll talk to Karen about colours and things. Should only take a couple of weeks.' Then, with one hand on her hip and the other caressing her throat, and a slightly sarcastic edge to her voice, she added: 'I do hope you can both wait that long.'

'Sorry to disappoint, Mum, but we won't be living downstairs. We'll find a place of our own, somewhere in the city if possible.'

'Oh, but, John, it would be so convenient for you to be here. You love it here; I know you do. Your father and I wouldn't interfere; you could come and go as you please.'

Her voice had taken on a desperate tone, her hand had moved from her throat and pressed against her chest in a dramatic pose. John could mentally feel her grip tightening around him.

'No, Mum, I don't think that would work for us. We'll start looking for a place in or near the city next weekend.' The steely edge to his voice should have warned her to stop right there.

'But you can't afford to live elsewhere, not before you graduate and get a job. Surely you're not proposing to live on Karen's wages. You'll end up in a hovel living on baked beans.' Obvious, naked desperation in her voice now.

This had also crossed John's mind, but he had a plan. Before another word was uttered, Ron snapped his fingers and, looking directly at Judy, exclaimed with glee, 'Just had an idea. Why don't they move into our apartment in the city? The last tenant moved out three weeks ago when their lease ran out and we haven't found a replacement yet.' He turned to John and smiled. 'I'll even throw in the first year rent-free. By then, you'll have graduated and will have a job. What do you say?'

John's plan had worked. He knew about the tenant moving out of his parents' apartment in the city and had timed his suggestion to Karen, and this conversation with his mother and father, to achieve this very outcome. Inside, he was elated, but he kept a lid on it until the deal had been done.

A look of annoyance set on Judy's face; she could see she was losing this argument. A few years ago, she'd gone to all that trouble to have the flat built downstairs so she could keep her eye on John. After all, he was her baby, and she liked to know where he was and what he was doing. Karen was a nice girl but not necessarily the one she would have picked for John, and now he was going to set up house with her. But before she could say another word, John hugged his father and laughed.

'Dad, you're a genius! That would be fantastic. Thank you so much for the offer, which we gratefully accept. It'll take us a couple of weeks to get set up, and then we'll have you and Mum over for dinner to celebrate. I'll ring Karen and tell her the good news.'

Judy's control over John and his future was slipping away. It was futile to try and argue further. She knew when Ron got an idea into his head, there was no stopping him. Deflated and exasperated, she put on a brave face and smiled. 'I hope it works out well for the two of you. You know we are always here, John, if you need us,' she said, pointedly omitting Karen from the last sentence. The inference had not escaped John's notice.

Excited and elated, John rang Karen to tell her the good news.

Karen's parents weren't happy about the move when she told them what was happening. They tried to explain that John was her first actual boyfriend and she should see a bit more of the world, and other men, before settling into a live-in relationship. Also, they didn't approve of couples living together before marriage. They realised more and more couples were doing it these days, but that didn't make it right. In their day, young people stayed at home until they got married.

Although she hated going against her parents' wishes, Karen was too besotted with the idea of living with John not to do it and they moved in together in the little apartment in the city.

Those first few years were blissful.

John graduated and secured a good job in a prestigious law firm. Karen decided paralegal work wasn't her vocation and secured a job in the office of a large advertising company in the city. She became friends with another girl, Miranda, who started working there the same day she did, and between the two of them, they ran the office and kept all the 'creative geniuses' happy. It was a fun place to work, although it became frantic and demanding whenever they were trying to win a new client, which, in those days, was often. But when the contracts were signed, the champagne would flow, and it would be celebration drinks in the office until all hours. John understood this was all part of her job and he, too, would often be late arriving home after long hours reviewing a case that was going to court the following day.

Whenever they had time to get lunch outside the office, Karen and Miranda would grab a quick sandwich together in the cafe next door to the office. The cafe was not far from the courts and occasionally John would join them for a coffee if he was in court. Sometimes, a friend of Miranda's, Kay, would join them for lunch. Kay worked at the Australian Tax Office, which was only a short walk to the cafe, and loved to hear what was going on in their office. It always sounded fun and exciting compared to where she worked. The Tax Office seemed very dull indeed when she heard about the things that happened in advertising.

Karen was living her dream. She had a great job which she loved, even if it was a bit mad from time to time. She was deeply in love with the man she was living with in a beautiful city apartment. Life was good.

3

LOSING JOHN

It had been a busy weekend—dinner with Judy and Ron on Saturday night, followed by lunch with Karen's mum and dad on Sunday. Karen had organised it so she could get an early night on Sunday in preparation for the breakfast meeting at the office scheduled for seven-thirty Monday morning. She liked to get into the office at least half an hour beforehand to get everything ready, and she knew Miranda would be there even earlier. Miranda had a work ethic like no other.

As far as friends go, Miranda was one of the best. She was always there when you needed her—like the day Karen organized the surprise birthday party for John in the apartment. Karen thought she could get everything ready in the morning and be in the office around one p.m., but things didn't go according to plan. It took so long to get everything finalised, she never made it into the office. Miranda covered for Karen—to such a degree nobody in the office even realised Karen wasn't at work.

Monday morning at seven-thirty, the meeting was up and running, finished by eleven-thirty. Karen had done the minutes and allocated relevant tasks, tidied up, and was making final checks with Miranda, all done by mid-afternoon.

'I think I might call it quits and take an early mark,' Karen said to Miranda. 'How about you?'

'No, I took one last week. Don't want to overdo it. You go. I'll take care of things here.' Miranda smiled as she blew Karen a kiss and ushered her out the door.

Gee, it's good to get away early occasionally, thought Karen as she walked home in the glorious spring sunshine. The morning's rain shower hadn't lasted long, and the clouds had cleared away by lunchtime, leaving the roads wet and glassy in the sun.

Hmm, pasta for dinner. I might even have time to make something for dessert. John probably won't be home until about six thirty. Might even pick up a nice bottle of red. She smiled to herself as she pushed open the door of the bottle shop and headed for the red wine section.

Fifteen minutes later, as she opened the door to their apartment, Karen heard a noise. It was a muffled sound, but she was instantly on guard as the apartment was normally so quiet. Beads of sweat broke out on her top lip as she called out, 'Is anyone there?'

'Yes, it's just me,' John replied as he walked up the hall from the bedroom. 'Please come and sit down. There's something I need to tell you.' Relief washed over Karen, thankful that it was only John and not a serial killer.

His voice sounded slightly different, almost hesitant, less distinct than usual. Confused and worried, thoughts raced through Karen's mind as she put her handbag on the kitchen counter and, still holding the bottle of wine, tried to work out what was going on. *What was John doing home at this time in the afternoon? Something bad must have happened. Had something happened to John's mother or father, or worse, her mother or father? Had something happened at John's office?* Judging by the look on John's face, it was bad news.

Nonplussed, she saw he was wearing casual clothes.

He took the bottle from her, placed it on the dining table, and led her to a lounge chair. She was now seriously concerned, and when he pulled one of the dining chairs over and sat down so they were facing each other, she felt panic rising in her chest.

'John! What's wrong? What's happened?'

'Karen, I don't know any other way but to say this but straight out. I'm leaving. I've met someone else.' He looked down at his shoes for a moment, then in the ensuing silence, he gathered himself together and brought his head back up to look her in the eyes. 'I'm leaving today.'

The overwhelming relief she felt when she knew nothing had happened to her parents only lasted a second or two before the revelation of what he had said began to sink in.

'What? What did you say?'

'I said, I'm leaving. Today. I've met someone else. Oh, Karen, I'm so sorry. It's taken me weeks to get the courage to tell you, but I've made up my mind. Since I met this woman, I've found out what love really is, what it's all about.

'We've had some great times together, Karen, but this is different from what I've felt for you these past few years. I tried not to get involved, but it was no use. I feel differently about her than I've ever felt before. I am so sorry.'

I can't believe he met someone else. When did it happen? How did it happen? Why did it happen? Where did he find the time? How could he do this to me? I don't believe it! Karen's mind spun—so many questions. She stared at him, wide-eyed, unblinking, incredulous. 'What are you talking about, John? How can you even think about leaving our life together? We are so happy here.'

'Please. Karen. Please try to understand.' He took a deep breath before going on. 'I, too, thought I was happy; we've had some wonderful times together. But when I met this other person, it was like a lightning bolt, love at first sight. She feels the same way. I'm sorry, Karen, but I've made up my mind. I'm leaving now. I've packed a couple of bags; they're in the bedroom.'

Then, almost as an afterthought as he rose and turned toward the bedroom: 'Oh, and Mum and Dad said you could stay in the apartment as long as you need. Don't feel you have to move straightaway. Take your time to decide what you want to do.'

Stunned disbelief became hurt, hurt became anger, and anger quickly became rage. Karen couldn't fathom what she was hearing. The fingers curled into fists and her nails dug into her palms, but it wasn't enough to stop her mind whirring. She could feel her legs trembling, could feel a hot sweat breaking out around her neck. *He probably thinks this offer from his parents would help soften the blow.* But this last piece of information was like petrol thrown on an already raging fire.

Karen stumbled after him as he walked towards the front door, a suitcase in each hand. She grabbed his arm and yanked him around to face her. 'What do you mean, your mother and father said!' She spat out the words as if they were poison in her mouth. 'Do you mean to tell me you discussed this with them before you said anything to me!?'

'Now, Karen, there's no need to be so angry.' John shook her hand off his arm. Karen could tell it hadn't even occurred to him that, by bringing his mother and father into this, it would make a bad situation worse.

'They're doing you a favour. I thought we could be grown up about this. I was hoping we could still be friends. I was hoping you could try to see it from my point of view, but it seems that's not possible.'

She ran along behind him as he strode to the front door and opened it, all the while trying to calm down, trying to think what to say next to stop her life from unravelling.

'John. John. We need to talk about this. Please, come back inside and let's talk. How did this come about? Why didn't you tell me you were unhappy?'

But he walked out and quietly closed the door behind him. The apartment was silent except for Karen's gasping breath and heaving sobs as the reality of the situation hit her.

The crying at last eased and when she could breathe normally, she went to the kitchen and poured herself a large glass of wine, took it to the comfy lounge chair near the window, flopped down, and began to think the situation through.

On reflection, Karen didn't know if she was more shocked that John had been seeing another woman, or that he had discussed it with his parents before he told her. How could he do that? Four years together, and he was still controlled by his mother. Karen shuddered when she thought about his mother—although she wouldn't say it out loud, she always thought John's mother was one to be wary of. *Might have dodged a bullet there, Karen.* At least the thought made her smile.

As she sat and sipped her wine, Karen contemplated what had happened. She could not get her head around the fact that this man she had known so intimately, so well, so lovingly, could have met somebody else, could have kept it from her, could simply walk away from everything they had together.

Her confusion and bewilderment turned inward on herself. How could she have not seen this coming? How could she have not suspected anything? How could she have been so wrong about him? What did this say about her judgment? Did she now need to question every other aspect of her life to see where else she could have been wrong?

Recalling every word of the conversation, she was amazed John had thought he could walk away from their relationship of nearly four years, and that they could remain friends.

Now, on her second glass of wine, Karen made the decision she never wanted to see or hear from him again. Ever.

By her fourth glass of wine, Karen thought she might possibly meet another man, someone she could get to know, and trust, over time. But she also knew she would never love another man the way she loved John.

That night was the longest night Karen had ever known. She drifted in and out of a fitful sleep, tossing and turning, hour after endless hour. Barely able to get out of bed, and unable to drag herself into work the next day, Karen caught sight of herself in the mirror in the hallway as she lurched towards the kitchen. The red eyes in the puffy, blotchy face stared back at her. She wiped one hand across her forehead and pulled the untidy, lanky hair back from her face. *I look as bad as I feel,* she thought, as she continued to the kitchen and picked up the phone. She rang Miranda and briefly filled her in on what had happened. Miranda had met John a few times and was as shocked as Karen was by his infidelity.

'Miranda, I really need to take a couple of days off. I'm no good to anyone at the moment. Please, could you let the boss know without going into too much detail?'

'Sure, leave it to me. And I'll be around to your place after work tonight with a bottle of wine. What you need is a friend and a drink!'

True to her word, Miranda arrived at the apartment around five-forty-five with a couple of bottles of wine. The two of them talked into the early hours, ordered in pizza, drank far too much wine, and when Miranda finally left, Karen sank into bed and slept a restless sleep, but sleep, nonetheless.

Over the following few days, Karen began to think more clearly through the haze of pain and subsiding anger. She hadn't heard from John, and she certainly wasn't going to contact him.

In the clear light of day four, she made a resolution to herself: *I will not let this breakup define the rest of my life. I will not let the past four years, and the end of what I thought was a lifelong relationship, turn me into a victim. From now on, I will say 'Yes' to any invitation, attend any function, dress to turn heads, and get on with my life.*

John hadn't died! He had decided he didn't want her anymore. His loss!

4

MEETING MARTIN

ON THE REBOUND

Karen met Martin within three weeks of the breakup, when Miranda's friend Kay introduced them. Kay and Martin were standing at the traffic lights waiting to cross Macquarie Street when Karen literally bumped into them while rummaging around in her bag for a tissue. *Damn these windy days; they always make my nose run.*

'Oh, hi Kay. Sorry, I didn't mean to bump into you. Wasn't looking where I was going.' Karen smiled her apology as she wiped her nose with a screwed-up ball of tissue.

'Oh, hello, Karen.' Kay smiled, unperturbed. 'We're on our way back to work after lunch.' Kay turned to the man beside her and, putting her hand on Karen's arm, said, 'Oh, Karen, this is Martin Cosgrove. He works at the Tax Office, same building as me. Martin, this is Karen Romano. Karen works with my friend, Miranda. You remember Miranda, my friend who works in advertising—where it's **exciting**!' Kay laughed as she rolled her eyes, emphasizing the word *exciting*.

By the time Karen and Martin had shaken hands and said the polite things people say when they're introduced, the pedestrian lights had turned green, and Kay and Martin waved goodbye to Karen and headed off across the busy road.

The following week, after obtaining her phone number from Kay, Martin rang Karen to ask her out for dinner. According to her resolve to say 'Yes,' she accepted. It had been four years since she'd been anywhere with a man other than John, and when the evening arrived, she thought to herself: *What the hell am I doing, going out with a strange man I know nothing about, a man I don't even know if I like? I must be truly desperate. Or stupid. Or both!*

Martin was polite, quite nice looking, and extremely well dressed, and to Karen's surprise, it turned out to be a pleasant evening. And although he didn't exactly sweep her off her feet, Karen agreed to go out with him again. She had forgotten how nice it was to be asked out, and even nicer to be taken to the types of places Martin suggested.

They continued to see each other every so often until gradually, dates with Martin became a regular occurrence. Karen and Martin became a couple who were known to be 'seeing each other exclusively,' and Karen's deep-seated hurt and unhappiness following the breakup with John began to recede. She found she could dispel the hurtful memory more easily and more often, thanks to Martin's care and affection.

Although Karen became fond of Martin, she was slightly dismayed when she realised he was getting serious about their relationship—he had fallen in love with her. Her mother and father thought he was a lovely man, even though he was quite a few years older than Karen. He seemed very respectful toward her, and after having seen her so unhappy after the breakup with John, her parents were quietly pleased she had met such a nice guy so soon.

Martin became a constant in Karen's life, always there whenever she needed anything, willing to go anywhere, anytime, to be with her. It concerned her that he seemed to be almost dependent on her for his very happiness, but it secretly flattered her that she had such power over another person. Martin had never been in a serious relationship before, and he was a bit like a rescue puppy who had found his forever home.

He was a good catch, and even though Karen wasn't in love with him, she became used to Martin being around. Plus, there was a certain charm in having an attractive man in love with you. What he lacked in passion, he made up for in dependability.

When conversation between the two of them turned to the future, marriage seemed to be the natural progression of things, and Karen was delighted with the two-carat diamond ring Martin gave her when they became engaged. Miranda was genuinely happy for Karen, thrilled she had left those feelings of the time she was with John behind, as were Mr. and Mrs. Romano. The happy couple were showered with gifts and best wishes, and when the time came for Karen to begin wedding arrangements, she became excited with the whole idea of a wedding and a future with Martin.

But in her quiet moments, when she was alone with her thoughts, she admitted to herself she wasn't in love with Martin, but perhaps, the feelings she had for him were what real life was all about—solid, dependable friendship.

Once this realisation set in, Karen viewed the future more realistically, rather than through rose-tinted glasses. Life married to Martin could be a good life—surely. It wasn't necessary to be in love with someone to make a good life with them. She only had to think about all the arranged marriages in the world today, so many of which lasted for as long as the partners were alive.

Maybe love could get in the way, cloud your judgment, allow you to become subservient to the other person. Karen made up her mind she was better off being realistic than being 'in love.'

She was not unhappy with her life, except she occasionally wished there could have been a bit more excitement here and there along the way. That risky, breathtaking, thrilling excitement some people experience in their lives.

She would love to have experienced that feeling, but in all the time she was married to Martin, she had never come close.

5

UNDERSTANDING MARTIN

When Eric Cosgrove returned home to Australia from the war in Europe in 1945, he decided he wanted a quiet life in the country, away from the city where the newspapers and radio seemed to do nothing but editorialize on the war and its repercussions and how it had affected Australia and Australians. He'd been home for about six weeks when he told his wife, Margaret, what he wanted to do.

'Marg,' he said. 'After being away from you for so long, fighting a bloody war in places you wouldn't want to know about, in conditions that were less than human, I reckon we deserve a decent life somewhere in the country where it's peaceful, and blokes aren't telling us what to do all the bloody time. I don't want to hear any more about the war; I'm trying to put it behind me. I don't ever want to see any of the blokes I fought with again; I don't want to be reminded.'

The mini outburst caught Margaret by surprise; Eric had always been so taciturn. She knew he'd been different since he came home, but she wasn't expecting this. It took her a minute to digest the information and decide the best way to handle it.

When Eric enlisted, Margaret continued to live in the little house they rented in Erskineville. She'd made some good friends in the area. The neighbours had helped her out several times while Eric was away, and she'd always felt comfortable living there. It wasn't a flash suburb, but it had a good community feeling about it.

During the years Eric had been away, Margaret had learned to fend for herself; had become proficient at doing things in the house without having to ask Eric's advice or permission. She had a good job in a factory within walking distance, and during the time Eric was away, she had done as she pleased. She'd missed Eric, but she had become used to being on her own and felt safe and secure with good neighbours close by.

She considered what Eric had said for a minute and thought: *A move to the country might short-circuit problems that could arise if he is continually reminded of what he went through.* Margaret had heard some terrible stories on the radio, and at work, about men who were never the same after the war, stories of families who broke up under the strain of men trying to come to terms with civilian life. Eric had given five long years to his country and his well-being was more important to their future than her self-centred life.

'I suppose that could work. What part of the country were you thinking of?' Margaret asked, as she peeled the potatoes for tonight's stew.

Eric leaned against the kitchen table as he watched her plop chunks of potato into the large, old, but much loved, pot on the stove. How he loved to watch her prepare food; it somehow gave him a sense of comfort and security whenever he watched her gather together things for a meal. She often told him she didn't enjoy cooking, but from his point of view, she seemed a natural. 'I hear they're looking for men to manage sheep stations out west, men who're prepared to work. I reckon I could run a sheep station. Would be good if we could find something out west.'

'Hmm.' Replied Margaret.

It didn't take long for Eric to find a job—as manager of the Southern Cross Station, a huge, remote, sheep property in far western New South Wales.

Although the heat was fierce and life wasn't easy, Margaret enjoyed running the manager's homestead on Southern Cross Station and kept it neat and tidy.

Within a few weeks of settling in, she embarked on a comprehensive first-aid course by correspondence. Although the station employed a cook for the men, first aid was the manager's responsibility. She ordered a first-aid kit, complete with hypodermic needles for various types of injections, antibiotics, and tourniquets for snake bite. Within weeks, she was a knowledgeable and astute nurse, on a first-name basis with the Royal Flying Doctor staff in Broken Hill.

Life was busy. There was always something going on. The enormous property required many people doing a wide variety of jobs to maintain it. There were always fences to repair, water tanks to mend, sheep to be dipped. It didn't take long for Margaret to learn to stand her ground with the station hands.

The men considered her a bit of a tyrant and secretly felt sorry for Eric.

A few months later, when they had finished unpacking all the crates and boxes in the homestead and had settled into a type of routine, one of the station hands, a wizened Aboriginal man by the name of Charlie, approached Eric one morning during Smoko.

'Hey, Boss,' he said shyly, as he removed his battered old Stetson hat and held it safely in both hands. 'How's Mrs. Boss goin', lookin' after the homestead? She need any help? My wife, Ellie, is lookin' for somethin' to do now the little ones're all growed up and left home. She's a good cook. Good cleaner too. She be big help to Mrs. Boss.'

'Ellie knows all about babies too,' Charlie added, smiling so broadly Eric thought his face might fall in half.

'I'll speak to Mrs. Boss and let you know tomorrow, Charlie,' Eric said. *Charlie's one of the best workers at the station—might be a good idea to keep him onside, especially if his wife's got the same work ethic.*

Later that evening, when Eric told Margaret what Charlie had said, she replied, 'I think it's a wonderful idea. I'd love to learn a bit more about Aboriginal culture, and it would be nice to have another woman around the house.'

Ellie was thrilled to be asked to work for the 'Boss Lady' and started work for Margaret immediately. A kind soul, Ellie was a good cleaner and cook, and did anything Margaret asked of her without hesitation. *Just like Charlie*, thought Eric when Margaret told him about her first couple of days with Ellie.

With Ellie's help, Margaret began to enjoy preparing wholesome and tasty meals. She'd never been much of a cook and had become even less proficient during the time Eric had been away at war. With more time on her hands, she sent away for the *Women's Weekly Cookbook* and set to making a variety of mouth-watering dishes. Eric had two station hands put in a water tank and make a garden near the homestead for Margaret, and she developed a productive vegetable and herb garden, as well as a few struggling roses. It was a tough life, but Margaret came to enjoy it. She was determined to make the most of their situation and never complained.

Both she and Eric were thrilled when their son, Tim, was born a year later. Ellie was overjoyed—a baby to look after! While she was pregnant, Margaret had sent away for books on pregnancy and parenting and felt reasonably prepared for what lay ahead. Tim arrived early, born about a week before his due date. Fortunately, the birth was relatively easy, and Ellie stayed by Margaret's side the entire time.

Tim was a delightful baby, placid and happy, and Margaret (and Ellie) loved having a baby to take care of. The size of the property was vast and sometimes Eric was away for long periods at a time. Even though Margaret had Ellie, it had been a lonely life for her at times. Now she had Tim to look after and fill her days with joy and love.

When Tim was nearly three, Margaret fell pregnant again, but this pregnancy was different from the first one. This time, she suffered severe morning sickness. Every day she would feel miserable and sick in the morning and, just as she was beginning to feel better, it would strike again in the afternoon.

Ellie tried everything she knew to make Margaret comfortable. The wretched nausea and vomiting eased off after the first three months, but as time passed, Margaret still felt something wasn't quite right. It was difficult to describe; it was only a feeling, but it made her apprehensive about the birth. She didn't like to worry Eric, especially right now when it was coming up to shearing time and he was so busy with running the station. But as the pregnancy progressed, she became more and more concerned.

One beautiful spring evening, they were sitting on the front porch, going over the events of the day and admiring the twinkling stars in the black velvet sky. Eric had poured a second glass of lemonade for Margaret and was organizing another whiskey for himself. *This would be a good time to talk about the baby, while he's feeling mellow from the whiskey and before he falls asleep in his chair.*

She sat up a bit straighter and sipped her drink before she began: 'Eric, this pregnancy is different from the first one. I don't feel so confident about the birth. What would you think if I booked into the hospital a couple of days before the baby's due? Ellie can look after things here. She would love to have little Tim to herself for a few weeks.'

Eric leaned forward and rested his elbows on his knees as he rolled the whiskey glass between his gnarled worker's hands, various thoughts running through his mind. The nearest hospital was a good hour's drive away. He placed his glass on the floor and straightened up before turning to Margaret and taking her hand in his.

'Why don't I ask Bob Sutton on the adjoining property if he can spare his wife for a few weeks? Jenny's a retired midwife; I reckon she'd jump at the chance to be with you for the birth. She and Ellie would make a formidable team. Their daughter's due back from the city to live with them in a couple of weeks, so it's not as if Bob would have to get by on his own. I'm sure you'd be more comfortable at home, and it would be easier for me.'

This hadn't occurred to Margaret, but now Eric mentioned it, it was a good idea. She would have been disappointed if Eric couldn't get to see the baby until it was two or three weeks old, which might be the case if she went to the hospital. She would certainly be more comfortable here at home too.

'Sounds like a good idea. Could you speak to Bob in the next day or two?'

Martin was born at home a few months later, and as Margaret had anticipated, it was a difficult birth. Thankfully, Jenny Sutton was on hand to help Margaret through the thirty-hour labour, which took its toll on both mother and baby. The baby struggled for breath at first and he was very small, but Jenny had encountered this before and knew the procedure to follow.

She tried to quell Margaret's rising panic about the baby. Margaret had lost a lot of blood during and after the birth and was weak. Jenny knew her anxiety about the baby would slow her recovery and tried to assure Margaret—and herself—all would be well.

'Try not to worry too much,' she said. 'We're doing everything possible for this little baby. Babies are a lot stronger than you might think.'

Jenny and Ellie worked tirelessly caring for Margaret and the baby—nothing was too much trouble to make both mother and baby as comfortable as possible. Three days after Martin was born, his colour had improved, and all three women were thrilled when Margaret was able to breastfeed him. Margaret was grateful to have Ellie there to look after Tim at this difficult time. She never forgot how Jenny had virtually saved her, and her baby's, life and would be forever grateful to this little woman with the kind face and indomitable spirit.

And because they nearly lost him, Martin would always and forever be 'the golden-haired boy.' He could do no wrong. As Margaret would often say, 'We are so lucky to have him. He is precious, and we must take good care of him.'

Margaret doted on Martin and spoiled him, to the boy's detriment. He grew up thinking he was a very special person with a very special place in the world. Although he was a nice-looking boy, his quick temper and sometimes demanding and abrasive manner didn't win him many friends.

The station under Eric's management prospered and in his second year, returned a profit for the first time in ten years. He'd had to learn about sheep classing, drenching, crutching, buying rams, lambing, fencing, and everything else it took to run a sheep station, very quickly. He'd made sergeant in the army during the war, which stood him in good stead in managing not just the property itself, but also the many station hands employed on a permanent or casual basis.

During the 1950s, Australia rode high on the sheep's back, and the price of wool increased exponentially. The owners of Southern Cross were extremely pleased with the results Eric had achieved and rewarded him accordingly. They bought the 96,000 acres of land adjoining Southern Cross Station and suggested he get his pilot's license as soon as possible. They bought him a small plane so he could cover the extended area more efficiently. Eric had fallen on his feet when he'd landed the job at Southern Cross Station. He didn't know if he could do it, but he was prepared to take the risk. With the right attitude and work ethic, he'd kicked every goal.

But the decision-making in any family situation fell to Margaret. As far as Martin and Tim could remember, she won every argument she ever had with their father concerning family matters. Their dad was a quiet man who loved his sons, but was a bit soft with the boys. Life was tough enough for him running a huge station, in charge of a lot of rough and tough men, without having to discipline his sons after a long day.

Margaret was a demanding woman and insisted things be done her way. It was easier for Eric to go along with whatever she wanted to do. Let Margaret look after the house and the boys—most of the time he was too exhausted at the end of each day to do anything but eat his dinner and fall into bed. The boys loved him, but he wasn't around a lot of the time, and they didn't get the opportunity to learn to appreciate what he did to keep them clothed and fed.

Tim was the one Martin looked up to: his role model. He watched everything Tim did, copied him, constantly sought his approval. When Tim spoke, Martin listened. He followed him everywhere, asked him endless questions—Why is the sky blue? Why do we have to have a bath every night? Where does the moon go during the day? Where's dad? And on and on and on. Tim was extraordinarily patient with Martin. He never complained and didn't seem to mind when Martin was never chastised or disciplined.

Tim was often blamed for things Martin did, like when they were playing cricket out behind the homestead and Martin hit the ball into the back-bedroom window and smashed it. Margaret didn't see who hit the ball, but it didn't stop her from running out of the house, shouting, 'Now look what you've done, Tim! You've broken the window! I told you to be careful when you're playing cricket with Martin. Go to your room.'

Tim knew better than to try to explain it wasn't him. She'd never believe it—Martin could do no wrong. And Tim knew Martin wasn't going to own up even though he knew he wouldn't get into trouble, so he did as he was told and walked up the back steps into the house while Martin followed him. Wherever Tim went, Martin went too.

Tim taught Martin how to chop wood for the fire, how to play marbles, how to train the dogs. It was Tim who jumped into the creek and saved Martin when he fell in; it was Tim who taught Martin how to swim. And when Martin was eight years old, Tim taught him how to smoke cigarettes—down behind the big water tank in the far paddock.

Because the Southern Cross Station was a remote property, both boys' early education was conducted via the School of the Air until the end of Tim's primary schooling. The discussion of what to do next about their schooling led to a serious argument between Eric and Margaret.

Even though she continued to dote on Martin, Margaret knew in her heart she needed to let him go, to untie the reins and let him find his own way in the world. She could see the boys needed to get out into the real world, to experience life beyond a sheep station. She also knew boarding school in Sydney would be a good springboard for their future careers—whatever they would be—and, as a mother, she wanted them to have the best opportunity possible.

But Eric argued the boys should finish their education on the property and learn how to run it. It was a large corporation now and would need astute men to oversee it one day. Eric had grown to love the station and had presumed the boys would one day take over from him. He wasn't getting any younger.

As usual, Margaret won the argument, and at the start of 1959—when Tim was thirteen, Martin ten—both boys were packed off to Cranbrook School in Sydney.

Tim settled in well to life at school. He enjoyed the routine, and it didn't take him long to make friends. He was a likable boy, well behaved and courteous, and he melded into the fabric of school life like a foot into a comfortable slipper.

Not so for Martin. He was used to getting his own way, having things done for him. Margaret had not set him up well for life in a boarding school. He was a very small fish in a very big pond at Cranbrook—nobody cared that he was a 'golden-haired boy,' and he was miserable for most of the time. He didn't understand why the other boys didn't include him in their groups, didn't want him on their sports' teams. He got the impression the teachers didn't like him much either. In Martin's mind, the others were always the ones at fault. He didn't think he was spoiled, abrasive, or rude. It was always the others with their misguided assumptions.

He found solace from his misery in study. In the library, or in a classroom after school hours, he found comfort in his books and enjoyed studying his beloved math and science lessons. When he concentrated on detail, he could shut out everything else in his life and learn and understand even the most complicated exercises. It was no surprise to his teachers when Martin repeatedly obtained the highest scores in any exam he took.

All the years he was at Cranbrook, Martin never learned to like the school, but he loved the learning. It satisfied him in a way nothing else had throughout his young life.

The school knocked the rough edges off the boys and taught them manners. Discipline was strict and education standards were high. Although both boys did well in their final exams, Martin topped the year and became Dux of the school. His mother and father and Tim were so proud of him. Eric and Margaret travelled to Sydney for his graduation and took the boys to dinner at Sydney's leading restaurant to celebrate.

'Would you like to invite some of your friends to come to dinner with us, Martin?' Margaret asked, smiling, and putting her arm around his shoulders in a warm embrace.

'I don't have any friends,' he replied without rancour. This didn't seem to bother him, but both his mother and his father were disappointed—although their younger son was academically clever, he hadn't learned the art of making friends.

Tim went on to Sydney University, where he graduated with a degree in Law. Martin went to the same university, and four years later, graduated with a degree in Economics, with Honours.

Neither of the boys returned to Southern Cross Station to live. They shared a flat in the city, and even though they enjoyed their occasional visits home to visit their parents and to stay in touch with the land, neither of them could wait to get back to the city and city life.

The two boys from the country had come to the city and found success in their chosen careers, a long way from a sheep station in western New South Wales. After Tim completed his law degree, he got a job with Rogers, Holt, and Hepworth, a renowned law firm in the city where he successfully completed a supervised traineeship after which he was admitted to the Bar and went on to secure his future with the firm as a contract lawyer. He was popular among the partners, diligent and hard-working, with a brilliant mind for the law. They were lucky to have him.

Martin applied for many jobs, but without success. His qualifications usually got him the interview, but his personality let him down. Interviewers didn't like it when the interviewee came across as superior, more worthy of the job than any of the other applicants. He possibly was more worthy, but employers usually preferred people who would fit in with the rest of their staff.

He was beginning to wonder what the future held for him when the Australian Tax Office in Sydney, to whom he had applied two months prior, wrote to him with a job offer. The job was poorly paid, at the bottom of the ladder, and one he felt over-qualified for—he was, after all, an Economics graduate, as he insisted on telling Tim.

Tim soon set him straight.

'Look, Martin, get over yourself! You're not that special. How many jobs have you got so far? None! So, you've got a degree. Big deal. So have I, and I had to do my time as a lowly law clerk before I was admitted to the Bar and started working in the law. Are you going to go on applying for jobs until you find the perfect one? It doesn't exist. Get real, Martin. Take the job, find out what it's like to earn a living. You never know, the Tax Office might be the making of you. You may even like it.'

He might regard other people's opinions with disdain, but Martin always respected Tim's. Instead of shouting an angry retort, he took a deep breath and considered hat he'd said.

With hands in pockets, and staring at the carpet, Martin muttered, 'You're always right, Tim. I'll accept the job.'

Martin had been at the Tax Office about 18 months when he was promoted to the fourth floor to work on corporation tax. He enjoyed this work; it was all about detail. He didn't have much contact with the other people in this division unless they needed some technical information, which Martin understood better than anyone. He learned everything he could about the tax system and the economy of the country and how they depended on each other. Even his superiors respected his opinion on technical tax issues.

In all the time Martin had worked at the Tax Office, he had never had a visitor, so he was nonplussed when Reception rang to tell him he had a visitor downstairs, that it was his brother, and could he please come down straightaway?

As he stepped out of the lift, Tim was waiting for him and led him to one of the empty ground-floor offices. Tim ushered him in quickly and quietly and closed the door. He pushed Martin gently towards a visitor's chair as he dragged the other one over so he could sit opposite Martin. Tim was aware his heart was racing, and he felt hot and sweaty even though the air-conditioning in this office was practically sub-zero.

'Sit down, Martin. I've got bad news.' A confused and anxious feeling seeped into Martin's stomach as Tim continued. 'The police contacted me at work to tell me there's been an accident out west involving Mum and Dad.'

Martin frowned as he put his hand on his forehead and sat stiffly upright in his chair. The heat of confused anxiety spread to the rest of his body, trickling down his legs; even his toes began to sweat. He felt extremely uncomfortable in the pit of his stomach. 'What? What's happened? How are they?'

'They were both on the plane when it went down. They're both dead, Martin. Both our parents are dead.' Tim slumped forward in the other chair and momentarily covered his face with his hands. He took in a gulp of air and said. 'I haven't been able to take this all in yet, but I know we both need to go home right now.'

Martin leaned forward and gripped the arms of his chair. 'Are you sure, Tim? I can't believe Mum and Dad are dead. How did it happen?'

'Apparently, they were on their way back from a barbecue over at Hardings' place near Broken Hill. They ran into bad weather and the plane went down in the middle of nowhere. It happened yesterday, but they didn't find the plane until this morning. The police came to my office to tell me, and I came straight here.'

Tim stood and put his hand on Martin's shoulder. 'Come on, mate, we've got to go home. There are arrangements to be made.'

'I'll have to go and let them know upstairs.' Martin appeared strangely calm on the outside, but he was shaking inside. He thought he was going to be sick.

'Don't worry about telling them upstairs. I've spoken to the girl on reception and she'll handle it.'

'What'll we do, Tim? What'll we do?'

'First, we'll go home.'

The two boys left the building and made their way home, Tim with his arm around his younger brother's shoulders.

True to his word, Tim made the necessary arrangements, and the boys left for Southern Cross Station later the same day. The funerals were held at Broken Hill within the week, and the boys began the arduous task of sorting through paperwork and going through their parents' things at the homestead. Their parents' solicitor in Broken Hill, Arnold Green, advised them of the contents of both wills and told them everything had been left equally to both boys.

Old Mr. Green sat behind his big leather-topped desk and removed his spectacles. He placed his elbows on the desk and looked compassionately at the boys.

'Your parents were both so proud of how you boys have turned out. To lose both parents together is a tragedy, but if anything had happened to either one of them, I don't know how the other one would have survived. They worked as a team for many years, each relying and depending on the other. They were devoted to Southern Cross Station and to each other. And remember, boys, irrespective of circumstances, the old cliché is true...life does go on.'

The brothers continued to live in the flat they shared in the city, but when the inheritance came through, they decided to buy an apartment in the Eastern Suburbs. After looking at various places, they eventually settled on a large three-bedroom apartment overlooking the harbour. The building was forty years old but recently renovated with no expense spared. A new lift had been installed and their apartment comprised the entire top floor of the building and came with two parking spaces. The living room had sliding glass doors leading out onto a sandstone patio with magnificent views over the harbour and out to the Heads. The three bedrooms were large, and the master bedroom suite had views of the harbour. The kitchen was spacious and well equipped. Not only was it a convenient place to live, but it was also a good investment for the future.

A year or so after they had settled into the new place Tim came home one night with a bottle of champagne and a big grin on his face.

'Guess what? I've been promoted!' he shouted, as he swung open the front door of the apartment with a dramatic sweep, holding a bottle of champagne high in his outstretched arm.

Martin came charging out of his room. He grinned when he saw the champagne being waved about in the air and exclaimed: 'Champagne! Must be a good promotion. Do I have to call you 'Your Honour' now?'

'I've been made a Junior Associate.', Tim laughed. 'I'm being transferred to the Head Office in Melbourne!'

'Melbourne!' Martin stopped dead in his tracks, his face stripped of all joy. 'Congrats on being made an Associate, but Melbourne? Don't they need Associates in Sydney?'

'Apparently not. But I'm happy to be an Associate at Rogers, Holt, and Hepworth anywhere.'

Martin was crestfallen. They had been together for many years now, from their days at Cranbrook, to their university days, to the flat they shared in the city, to their current home in the Eastern Suburbs.

'Gee, Tim, I'll miss you. I'm delighted about the promotion, but I wish it wasn't in Melbourne.'

'I'll miss you, too, mate,' Tim said, putting his arm around Martin's shoulder. 'But I think it'll be a good thing for you to live your life independent of me and make your own way in the world.'

Martin thought about this for a moment. Maybe living on his own would be a good thing. He knew he was a bit of a fusspot, always complaining about Tim being untidy. Now he'd be able to keep the apartment pristine.

The idolatry he held of his big brother as a kid had never dulled but had instead matured into respect and admiration.

'You're right, Tim. You always are.'

Martin took the champagne bottle from Tim and began to tear off the wrapper. 'Let's get into this champagne, then I'll shout you to dinner somewhere flash to celebrate my brother, the Associate!

Four weeks later, Tim had packed up, moved out, and was on his way up the ladder of success as a Junior Associate at the Melbourne Head Office of Rogers, Holt, and Hepworth, one of the finest law firms in the country.

The apartment seemed a bit bare now Tim wasn't leaving his detritus everywhere for Martin to tidy up, but it didn't take long for Martin to appreciate the benefits of living alone. Now, the beautiful old apartment always looked like something out of a decorator magazine—beautifully furnished, spotless, tidy. Anytime Martin felt lonely, he used his old trick of devoting himself to work. This paid double dividends—it kept him focussed and flat-out busy, and, as a result of his conscientiousness, he was promoted to the fifth floor, the Law Design and Practice Division.

Life for Martin settled down to a comfortable routine. He developed a habit of swimming with the Bondi Icebergs at Bondi three or four mornings a week before work. He played tennis every Wednesday evening at the well-kept courts within walking distance of the apartment. Two of the fellows at tennis also played golf once a week and invited Martin to join them. Although he was a complete novice at the game, he soon became a regular with the same group of men every Sunday. Over time, his game steadily improved and he eventually got his handicap down to twelve.

About a year after he'd settled in Melbourne, Tim rang one weekend with the news he had become engaged to a great girl—a colleague's sister. He told Martin they planned on getting married in about six months and asked Martin to be his best man. Martin was genuinely pleased Tim had found happiness and was delighted to be his best man at the wedding—where he made a wonderful, heartfelt, and sometimes very funny speech wishing the bride and groom a long and happy married life together.

During the following eight or nine years, Tim and Sue produced four children. Martin travelled to Melbourne four times a year to see the family. It was clear he adored his niece and three nephews. The bond between Tim and Martin lost none of its strength, even though they lived in different cities, and Martin loved visiting Tim and Sue and the kids. Every time he visited, Sue would invite one or more of her single girlfriends along to various social gatherings she organized so Martin could meet available women, but he had never been particularly interested in girls, or a social life outside of sport, so it was invariably futile.

In the ten years he'd been at the Tax Office, Martin hadn't made any real friends at work. Occasionally he was invited to join the fellows from the fifth floor for a drink after work, but he felt like an outsider in this clique. He wasn't good at being a friend—his sometimes abrasive manner tended to put people off. Curiously, he got on very well with the women in the various divisions where he'd worked. He had never had a girlfriend as such but had been more popular among his female colleagues than with any of the men. He would occasionally join a couple of them for coffee or lunch at the café near the office.

One day, he rang down to the third floor and Kay answered. Kay ran the Archives section and was smart and funny. Even though Kay would have been ten years younger than Martin, they enjoyed a good rapport and he loved her razor-sharp wit. They both enjoyed having lunch together occasionally.

'Hi, Kay, doing anything for lunch today?' he asked casually. 'Thought I'd go to the café over the road. Want to come?'

'Sounds like a good idea. I didn't have time to make myself anything for lunch this morning, and I'm starving. How about we meet downstairs at about twelve thirty?'

The café was crowded, but they managed to find a tiny table and two seats outside on the footpath. Even when it was crowded like this, the service at the café was fast and cheery. Their sandwiches and coffees arrived in no time and were delicious, as always.

'The food here is always good, don't you reckon,' Martin said as a statement, more than a question.

'It sure is,' Kay replied. 'Mind you, I was so hungry I would've eaten anything.'

They chatted as they drank their coffee, and at about 1:50, Kay looked at her watch. 'Well, I'd better get back to the office. I stayed a bit later last night so I don't feel bad taking a little extra time over lunch, but I don't want to overdo it.'

'Yes, I didn't realise that was the time,' Martin said as he took some notes from his wallet and placed them on the table with the bill. 'My shout. You can get the next one.'

'Thanks, Martin. I will.' Kay replied as they left the café and headed off along Macquarie Street towards the traffic lights at the next major intersection. As they were waiting for the lights to change to green, Kay was almost knocked over by another woman, who was most apologetic.

'Oh, hello, Karen.' Kay smiled as she recognized the woman. 'We're on our way back to work after lunch.'

Kay turned to Martin and, putting her hand on Karen's arm, said, 'Oh, Karen, this is Martin Cosgrove. He works at the Tax Office. Martin, this is Karen Romano. Karen works with my friend, Miranda. You remember Miranda, my friend who works in advertising—where it's *exciting*!' Kay laughed as she emphasized the word *exciting*.

Martin and Karen exchanged pleasantries, and the conversation was developing when the lights changed to green. Kay and Martin waved their goodbyes as they hurried off across the busy road.

Kay was chatting away to Martin as they approached the entrance to their office building, but he didn't hear a word she said. His mind was slightly muddled, trying to work out why a woman he had just met would make such an impression on him. He had never been a ladies' man, hadn't ever thought about a wife and family—his life revolved around work and sport, and that had always suited him. But now he was confused as a completely unrecognised feeling washed over him and he realised he wanted to see her again.

As they pushed their way through the revolving door into the foyer of the building, Martin stopped. He looked at Kay and said, 'Sorry, Kay, my mind was elsewhere. What were you saying?'

Later in the afternoon, Martin took the lift down to the third floor and looked around for Kay, finding her at the tea urn in the staff kitchen.

'Hi, Kay, I was wondering...that woman you introduced me to at the traffic lights, Karen Romano, I think was her name...would you have her phone number? I'd like to contact her.'

'Pardon me?' said Kay in disbelief, very nearly pouring boiling water over her hand. *Did he just ask for a woman's phone number?* She thought she must have misheard him.

'Have you got Karen's phone number?' The urge to tap his foot was strong, but he resisted.

'Oh, sorry, Martin.' She paused for a moment as she placed the kettle back on the stove, a perplexed look on her face. 'I didn't think you went out with girls. We always thought you were a loner, maybe even gay.' Kay smiled as she spoke, and gently touched Martin's arm. 'No offense, Martin, but I didn't think you were interested in women.'

'No offense taken, but I thought Karen was rather nice.' He couldn't help mimicking Kay's turn of phrase.

'She is. I'll get her number for you now.' Kay found her address book and copied out Karen's phone number on a slip of paper for him. She shook her head in disbelief as he walked away, smiling.

Such was his fear of rejection, it took Martin a week to get up the courage to phone Karen. He practiced the conversation in his head over and over and prepared an answer for at least five different replies Karen could possibly make when he eventually asked her out. He was not good at this. *Damn, I wish I'd had more practice. I'd be a lot more confident if I'd done this before,* he thought as he picked up the phone. *Thirty-four years old and scared to ask a woman out on a date—what an idiot!*

He had hardly been able to stop thinking about her since Kay had introduced them. No woman had ever affected him like that before—she seemed different, quietly self-confident; she listened when he spoke, not like most other people who lost interest in what he was saying long before he'd finished saying it. It was the briefest of conversations at the traffic lights, yet he kept hearing her voice in his head.

So, on Wednesday night, he phoned her. And she answered. And he asked her out. And she accepted! He was elated, and although he tried not to overthink the coming date, he couldn't concentrate on anything else for the rest of the evening.

Don't get too excited, he told himself. *Anticipation is always better than the actual event.*

But the actual event was wonderful, better than any dinner he'd ever been to. He took her to the five-star, expensive restaurant at the Opera House, and they had a superb meal and some high-priced wine, none of which he could remember later. All he could recall was Karen, and how she looked, and smelled, and smiled, and spoke, and listened. He was completely infatuated after one date.

But he told himself not to rush her. It's what Tim had always said. *Don't rush them—women like to be courted.*

Well, he could do that.

The following day, he went to Percy Marks, the best jewellers in the city, and bought the most beautiful glittering two-carat diamond ring in the store—a solitaire diamond set in a plain gold band.

After one date, Martin knew he wanted to marry Karen, but he was prepared to wait for the right moment to make his move. And he did.

6

AN EXCITING NEW VENTURE

Karen and Martin had been married for nearly five years when their son, Tony, was born. The pregnancy did not go smoothly. The morning sickness, often experienced for the first three months, lasted the full nine months and Karen was glad to give up work, even though she knew she would miss the buzz and the people, especially Miranda. When she left the advertising agency five months before the baby was born, the agency gave her a huge send-off party. During those months before Tony arrived, Karen and Martin had both agreed Karen would be a stay-at-home mum.

Life as a nonworking mother suited Karen; she loved watching Tony grow into a cheeky toddler and before she knew it, he had started school at Martin's alma mater. She enjoyed taking Tony to and from school and made friends with many of the other mothers on the school run. They organised morning teas and lunches and she always had something to do, to look forward to.

However, when Tony entered high school, she found she had more time on her hands. He'd leave for school at eight each morning, and most days, wouldn't get home before about five in the afternoon. Some days seemed to drag, and Karen even found herself bored one day. That was the day she began to think about going back to work. The more she thought about it, the more it seemed like a good idea. But then she realised an even better idea would be to start some sort of business, especially one where she could tailor her hours to suit their lifestyle.

Karen had never been much of a cook, but she loved all the accoutrements of cooking and owned every possible kitchen and cookware tool. Martin often joked they could open a store with all the cooking gadgetry in the pantry. Since Tony had started high school, she found herself spending more time in kitchen shops, which was when the idea occurred to her: *I could open a kitchenware store.*

After much research, and checking out virtually every kitchenware shop in Sydney, she was convinced she could do it better. She had even found the perfect place. Now all she needed was the right time to tell Martin.

She didn't have to wait long. The following Sunday, the two of them sat out on the terrace over-looking the harbour on a perfect Sydney weekend, enjoying a leisurely breakfast of croissants and coffee. Tony was off down the beach with his friends and Martin was reading the Sunday papers as usual, relaxed and comfortable.

Mmm, this would be a good time to tell him, thought Karen, as she reached for another croissant.

'Martin, I've been thinking…'

Without looking up, Martin turned the page of the Sports section, shook out the creases in the paper, and absent-mindedly murmured: 'Hmmm?'

'I'd like to open a kitchenware shop. You know I love all that sort of stuff. You've always joked I've got enough things in the pantry to start a shop.' With no reaction from the other side of the table, Karen leaned over and topped up Martin's coffee cup from the fresh pot as she ploughed on.

'I've found some vacant premises in a great spot in the main shopping strip of Woollahra. It's a bit larger than I need, but I reckon it's always better to have too much room than too little. What do you think?'

Still no reaction. A minute, maybe two, passed in silence before Karen blurted out, 'Come on, Martin. Say Yes.'

Martin looked up at last and as he reached for his coffee cup, replied. 'As long as it doesn't interfere with my routine, and doesn't become a drain on our finances, I don't see why not.' He turned another page of the Sports section, shook the creases out, and buried his head in the paper.

Oh, don't worry, it won't interfere with your precious routine, thought Karen, *and thanks for your encouragement and support.*

Karen signed a lease on the shop the following day and immediately started organizing builders and carpenters to turn her idea into a reality.

Most of the kitchenware stores Karen had been in were very bright, very modern, and with very little character. Karen wanted her store to look warm and welcoming, cosy and inviting.

The first thing she did was to install an imitation worn-looking stone floor. Three walls were painted a pale sage green, which beautifully set off the displays of dinner sets and shiny cutlery. The builders chipped away the plaster on the back wall exposing the original old, dark brown speckled bricks—perfect for displaying a range of artwork depicting food and kitchen equipment. Suspended from the centre of the ceiling, and running the full length of the shop, the builders fixed a rack from which hung a variety of highly polished copper saucepans and frying pans. Downlights in the high ceiling made the stock sparkle and shine.

A section at the back of the store was partitioned off and turned into an office where Karen installed her computer and office paraphernalia.

Time to find staff! Karen hired the first woman she interviewed, who turned out to be an absolute gem—loyal, hardworking, and as a bonus, a wonderful cook. It took her a bit longer to choose the other four women, as she wanted employees who actually used most of the goods they stocked, who knew and understood about cooking and cooks.

Only one man replied to the advertisement, and when Karen interviewed him, she hired him on the spot. He was a young gay guy with a great flair for display, who was also a good cook. He helped Karen decide on uniforms for all of them—long black skirt or slacks, crisp white shirt with a green cravat, and green-and-white-checked gingham apron. Karen was happy to supply the uniforms. It was important to the overall look of the store and critical that everyone look neat, tidy, and efficient.

And so, The Cookery Nook opened its doors and the customers flooded in, curious to investigate this new and interesting-looking shop in the heart of trendy Woollahra.

Once she had fully stocked the shop and had the business up and running, Karen discovered her true calling: she was a natural businessperson—from negotiating rent and conditions, to hiring the right staff, to purchasing stock she knew would sell, to charming customers and sales reps alike to secure the best deal. The shop was successful from the day it opened, thanks to the decor, the variety of kitchen appliances and cookware, and Karen's ability to engage with staff and customers.

One Monday morning, as Karen checked appointments in the diary for the coming week, she noticed one appointment made by Denise, her best saleswoman. She called Denise over and showed her the diary.

'Denise, this isn't Lou Bristow, the chef, is it?' she asked, pointing to the name in the book.

'It absolutely is,' replied Denise, beaming as she thrust her hands into her apron pockets. 'I couldn't believe it when he rang last week to make an appointment with us. To make doubly sure, I asked him directly if he was the chef, Lou Bristow, and he said yes, he was, and if he could please make an appointment to call on our shop. So, you're seeing him on Thursday.'

Denise stopped to draw breath, and Karen smiled. Denise looked like the new puppy who had returned with the ball in his mouth after having retrieved it from under a bush. She was so obviously chuffed she herself had made the appointment, even though it was he who had rung them.

Lou Bristow was well known around town as a top chef who had been working for one of Sydney's leading restaurants for a few years now.

Denise went on excitedly: 'I can't wait to meet him, and perhaps pick his brains about souffles.' During her interview with Karen, she had mentioned she was a passionate cook, but in all her years of cooking, had never been able to master the art of souffles.

On Thursday, Lou arrived at the appointed time, dressed in a collar and tie, and carrying a large suitcase. Denise's heart fell—not exactly the image she had in mind of a great chef, but he certainly was a good-looking man. She thought she had read somewhere he was in his mid-forties.

'I'll let Karen know you're here, Mr. Bristow. She's just out the back; she won't be long.' And, stifling a giggle, she scurried away to the office to tell Karen.

'He's here, but I don't think he's here as a chef,' said a disappointed Denise, thrusting her hands into her apron pockets.

Karen peeked through the one-way glass between the office and the shop to get a look at Lou Bristow before she met him. Wow, he was certainly a lot better looking than he appeared in the newspaper photos she'd seen of him. He was tall, slim, well dressed, and standing straight, but relaxed.

Karen put on her best businesslike persona and checked herself in the small mirror which hung on the back of the office door before she walked out of the office. She introduced herself to Lou, who shook hands and handed her his card:

Lou Bristow
Sales Representative
Yamamato Knives
Japan
The World's Finest Knives

Mmm, interesting. There's obviously a story behind this turn of events, Karen thought, as she turned and led him through the shop.

'Come into my office and we'll have a cup of tea and you can tell me all about yourself, and these wonderful knives.'

Over the next hour or so, Lou told her all about his career and where it had taken him.

He had always loved cooking, even as a child, and had studied and qualified as a chef twenty years ago. He had worked at various cafés and restaurants in the suburbs, steadily gaining experience and learning the tricks of the trade. Then about four years ago, he had been approached by the owner-chef of Sydney's leading restaurant who had offered him a job working under him in the restaurant. Lou jumped at the chance; it was a coveted position and one any up-and-coming chef would grab with both hands.

It was hard work from the get-go, but he told himself how lucky he was to be learning from a master. After all, how many people got an opportunity like this? This was what being a *real* chef was all about: demanding, strenuous, long hours, perfection, budgeting, understanding financials, being on call at all hours of the day and night. However, he hadn't realised the man he was working for was a dictator of mammoth proportions.

Eventually, the pressure got to him, and after several discussions with his wife and family, he opted for a less stressful life and quit, intending to enjoy a break and to take his wife overseas for a well-earned holiday.

Karen realised this would have been a difficult decision for a five-star chef such as Lou Bristow.

Lou relaxed as he told his story and continued:

'The Japanese knife company Yamamato contacted me immediately. They had heard I'd left the restaurant and offered me the job of sales director of their Australian division at a substantial salary and benefits. They knew I'd been using their knives for many years.

'I don't know if you're familiar with Yamamato, Karen, but they make their knives using a new-alloy steel which is able to be sharpened like carbon steel, but with a mixture of molybdenum and vanadium—makes the steel more resistant to rust. They're made to the most exacting standards and specifications; the blade is ground to a narrower edge than most, so it is thinner, and the handles are hollow and filled with sand. Their standard of quality makes then expensive, plus they require special instruction in their use and care—something I'm familiar with as I've used them for years throughout my career as a chef.'

Lou stopped for a breath and smiled, embarrassed, but Karen could see he was genuine in his enthusiasm about the company he now worked for.

'Love your passion for your product,' said Karen. 'It looks like you're enjoying what you're doing now so much more than working in the pressure-cooker conditions of a five-star restaurant.'

'I think we can do good business together.'

7

TRUE FRIENDS

Karen liked Lou Bristow from the first time they chatted, and he soon became her favourite salesperson. She often sought his advice on many of the other items she stocked in the shop, which he happily gave. He was a pleasant and obliging man, and they developed a deep and meaningful business relationship. Karen respected him as a person and a supplier, and never failed to tell Lou how much she appreciated his help.

Due to the sales prices of the Yamamato knives, they were not easy to sell. Lou had been calling on the shop for about a year when Karen rang him and asked him to come and see her. It was usually the salespeople who rang to make an appointment with the retailer, but she had an idea she wanted to discuss with Lou and couldn't wait for him to call next month. She was too excited to wait, but apprehensive at the same time—what if he was insulted when she put her idea to him? What if he didn't think it was a good idea? What if his bosses thought her idea was beneath their sales director's status?

'Lou, hi, come into the office; there's something I want to talk to you about.' Eyes sparkling, cheeks flushed, an air of expectation fluttered about her like a butterfly as she tugged on his sleeve and drew him into the office.

'This better be good,' Lou said with a laugh. 'I was on my way to David Jones to break my monthly sales record.'

Once they were seated at her little desk in her office, she started talking. 'I had this idea. What if we cleared an area in the shop and set up a butcher's block and cutting boards, special cuts of meat, vegetables, etcetera, etcetera, and you did a demonstration of how to use the Yamamoto knives? We could do ads in the local paper and on the radio. I reckon we could increase the sales of your knives. What do you reckon?

Lou smiled his charming smile, leaned over the desk, and shook her hand. 'That's a great idea! When?'

Karen visibly relaxed, positively beaming. This was going to be good. 'I worked out I can organise the advertising and set everything up within two weeks.'

Her enthusiasm was contagious, and Lou caught some of her excitement. 'How about we do a Thursday night, say, six o'clock? We could get women on their way home from work and your regular customers.'

'That's a great idea. I'll organise everything for Thursday of next week.'

Karen organised an advertisement in the local paper featuring a photo of Lou, and described him as 'the famous chef, Lou Bristow'. The ad stated: 'Lou will be demonstrating his skills with Yamamoto knives, the finest in the world, and giving personal instruction on their use and care. Come along and discover why they are both 'the best in the business'.' She reprinted the ad in a brochure and did a letterbox drop in the area.

Late on the Thursday afternoon, Karen called Denise over. 'Come on, Denise, help me move some of the displays. We need to make enough room to squeeze in the butcher's block and about ten chairs.'

Denise was thrilled to be included in this promotion. She had been enthusiastic about it from the moment Karen had explained it to her and didn't doubt for one moment it would be anything but a huge success. This was one of the reasons Karen paid Denise considerably more than the other employees in the shop—her ability to always see the positive side of any situation was worth more than money to Karen.

Karen, not as blindingly optimistic as Denise, hoped they would get ten customers, but what if nobody came? Oh well, there were a few bottles of champagne in the fridge in the office so they could always drown their sorrows.

Lou arrived at five thirty to help the girls complete the setup, and by six p.m. all was ready. The sandwich board notice had been placed on the pavement outside the shop entrance and the first customers began to arrive.

Karen smiled as she welcomed the first guests—her next-door neighbours, two gay fellows who were both good cooks and regular customers. Karen loved them for their unwavering support and their cheeky sense of humour.

'Hi, guys, it's lovely to see you. Thank you so much for coming. Let me introduce you to Lou. Lou, these lovely gentlemen are my next-door neighbours, Freddy and Wolfie.'

The men shook hands. 'We are so thrilled to meet you, Lou. We've read so much about you over the years. And we love your recipes, don't we, Wolfie?' Freddy exclaimed, blushing.

Lou beamed and showed them to the two front seats as Wolfie whispered, 'Love your loafers, by the way, Lou.'

They were followed by three women, who were quickly joined by another four or five couples. The seats were all taken, and the shop was filling up fast. As Karen glanced around the shop, taking it all in, she counted at least twelve more people standing, as well as the ten customers who had made use of the chairs. She caught Lou's eye and mouthed, 'Time to start the demonstration,' as she gave him the thumbs-up sign with both hands and a glowing smile.

'Good evening, folks. So glad you could come tonight.' Lou smiled as he picked up one of the largest knives in the Yamamato range and began.

He talked for over an hour, with not one dull minute. He was perfect, combining the right amount of humour with serious knowledge of knives and how to use them properly, and the little crowd loved him. Freddy and Wolfie listened spellbound, hanging on Lou's every word.

The evening was a spectacular success. They sold more Yamamato knives on the night than they had since they'd started stocking them. The customers loved Lou, and he enjoyed the direct interaction with the consumers who would be using his products. Karen had planned on being out of the shop by eight o'clock, but they ushered out the last customers, Freddy and Wolfie, at about nine thirty. It was only then they were finally able to close the door. The evening had been fun and profitable, and Karen was delighted.

'What do you reckon about doing this again next month?'

Lou laughed. 'What a great idea!'

And they did—the following month, and every month for the next year.

Three months after the first demo, Lou casually suggested if Karen could get a two-burner portable stove and a few ingredients, he could not only demonstrate the knives, but he could cook up a couple of things to make it more interesting.

'What a great idea!' said Karen.

'That's what I thought,' said Lou.

And they laughed and laughed, the laughter of success.

And so, their monthly 'Knives and Cooking Demonstrations' became an event well known around town, and the sales increased. It was a golden time for the business, and everyone benefited. They knew it wouldn't last forever, but they also knew it was a 'great idea' for however long it lasted.

Karen was thrilled when Lou asked her and Martin to dinner at his place to meet his wife, Carole. They were not disappointed.

Carole was delightful, a naturally upbeat person, full of the joy of life. She looked to be around the same age as Lou, naturally attractive without the need for heavy makeup, with dark mid-length hair. She wore black slacks and a white linen blouse, which suited her figure. Not only did they make a good-looking couple, but Karen could see they were obviously well suited and happy in each other's company.

After Lou made the introductions, Carole led Karen and Martin into a stylishly decorated living room and opened a bottle of champagne while Lou finished up in the kitchen. When Lou joined them a few minutes later, the four of them sat and chatted until it was time to move into the dining room.

Lou and Martin hit it off from the start. They shared a love of cooking, although Martin quickly made the point he wasn't, and never would be, in Lou's class. Dinner was superb—the most amazing crispy-skinned roast duck with an orange, cranberry, and cinnamon sauce served with caramelised Brussels sprouts, followed by homemade caramel ice cream with a rich sticky sauce.

Karen and Carole glanced at each other and smiled at the unusual sight of two grown men sitting over dinner, discussing recipes and talking food in great detail, oblivious to the others, while enjoying the delicious red wine Martin had brought as they compared pan frying to grilling, gas to electric, and the value of using ingredients as fresh as possible.

During the car ride home, Karen and Martin talked about what an enjoyable evening it had been and how it was not often they got to spend an evening with such pleasant people who seemed to be genuinely happy with each other.

'I'd like to ask them over to our place in the next few weeks. What do you think, Martin? You could do the cooking.'

'I don't think that's such a great idea. I would feel very intimidated by Lou. I'd probably botch it up.'

'Martin, I don't think you realise what a nice person Lou is, or how good a cook you are. He would never embarrass you. As a matter of fact, he'd probably love it if you picked his brains for some useful tips and tricks. I reckon he and Carole would love to come over.'

Karen looked across at Martin to gauge his reaction. The way he was frowning meant he was either concentrating on his driving—which was a good thing—or he still wasn't comfortable cooking for Lou and Carole. Karen had known Martin for a very long time and had learned the best way to convince him of anything was to just talk. She leaned over and changed the station on the car radio. Soft classical music oozed out of the speakers as she began. 'Did I tell you what happened last week while Lou was showing me the latest knives from Japan?'

'No, you didn't.'

This was the opening she needed. She could now reel him in with her anecdote.

'Well, the shop was exceptionally busy, and full of customers. The girls were handling them as best they could, but as fast as one customer left, another two came in.'

'Martin, it was the busiest I have ever seen the shop. When I excused myself to go and take care of some of the customers, Lou offered to help in the shop until the rush had died down. I was so grateful. Martin, he was in his element, interacting with the customers as he made sales of some of his beautiful, and expensive, knives. He's a natural salesman: diplomatic, charming, cheeky, helpful. The customers absolutely loved him. I can assure you Martin, Lou would never intimidate you.'

'You're probably right. Let's do it.'

When Lou and Carole came over for dinner at Karen and Martin's, Martin excelled himself with the meal, and the success of the dinner boosted his ego for days. Lou was genuinely impressed with Martin's cooking and even suggested a couple of alternate ways to achieve the same end with less work by the cook. Martin couldn't even find anything to complain about. The fact he was in awe of Lou meant Martin kept a lid on his usual criticism of anything and everything.

The social aspect of Karen and Lou's relationship didn't get in the way of their business dealings—both Karen and Lou were too professional to compromise what was, for both, a remarkably successful and ongoing business arrangement.

Following such an enjoyable couple of dinners, a type of loose arrangement was made to get together for dinner at each other's homes every month or so.

Business was good for several years and both Karen and Lou prospered. During this period, Karen had one of her best weeks ever. The shop looked wonderful and the customer database was increasing in leaps and bounds. Takings were up, and she was riding on the crest of a wave. Lou and Carole were coming to dinner on Saturday night, and both Karen and Martin were looking forward to it. Martin was doing a slow-roasted shoulder of lamb with baked Mediterranean vegetables and a special sauce—the recipe for which had been provided by Lou several months ago. He couldn't wait to see what Lou thought of it.

That afternoon, as Karen sat at the kitchen counter chatting with Martin, who was up to his elbows in peeled vegetables and oil, the phone rang. Karen stretched over to the phone handset on the wall and lifted the receiver.

'Hello. Karen Cosgrove speaking.' Immediately, she knew it was Lou and something was wrong.

'I'm sorry, Karen, but we're not going to be able to make it for dinner at your place tonight. Carole is not well. I'm very worried about her. She's been tired for a few weeks now and has complained of stomach pain for a few days. She's even been sick a couple of times today. She doesn't look good either—her eyes are not white like they usually are. I'll take her to the doctors on Monday.'

'Oh, I'm really sorry to hear that, Lou. We'll miss you guys tonight. Please keep me informed of how she is.'

Martin had heard the brief conversation and tried to hold back his disappointment. As it turned out, the dinner was fabulous, but there was an awful lot left over.

Lou had an appointment with Karen in the shop the following Wednesday, but when he didn't show, she became worried Carole may still be sick. When she hadn't heard from him by the Friday, she rang his mobile. He answered immediately and sounded terrible.

'Oh, Karen, I'm sorry I haven't been in touch. I've been flat out this week taking Carole for tests. She's much worse than any of us imagined. She's been diagnosed with pancreatic cancer and her prognosis is not good....' He hesitated over the last few words and broke down.

Karen could feel the blood drain from her face as her hand automatically went to her throat. 'Oh, Lou, I am so sorry. She seemed fine the last time we saw you guys. How could something like that happen so quickly? What a shock; you must be distraught. Is there anything we can do?'

The funeral was a very sombre and sad affair. Carole was only forty-seven and so full of life, a wonderful wife and mother—it wasn't fair someone with so much to live for should have their life cut short. Their two boys each gave a beautiful eulogy, but Lou was too distressed to speak. It was all he could do to thank the mourners as they offered their condolences. He looked dreadful and felt even worse. How could he face the rest of his life without Carole, his first and only love, to whom he had been married for 26 wonderful years?

Lou returned to work within a couple of weeks, but Karen could see it was going to take a long time before he regained any of his joie de vivre. Karen and Martin continued to have him over for dinner every few weeks and Lou returned the favour. The evenings were difficult at first, the fun and laughter Carole had brought to the table sadly missing. But as time passed, Lou began to accept the new normal for him. He had to find a new way of living without Carole. No matter how hard he wished, she wasn't coming back. His sons visited often and were a significant support to him, but he knew he could not become reliant on them for his life outside of work.

Karen and Martin made a determined effort to support Lou, aside from the times he called on Karen at work or when the three of them had dinner together. Martin would phone and ask Lou to go for a drink, and on these occasions, they would chat over a beer about politics, football, cars, and other impersonal subjects. Karen often phoned him to see how he was doing, and Lou found he could talk to Karen about more intimate stuff—feelings, sleepless nights, his boys, and how much he missed Carole.

A few years after Carole's death, Karen and Martin were at Lou's for dinner one evening, when Lou made an announcement that caught them unawares.

As usual, they were sitting in the living room drinking champagne, making small talk and enjoying the ambience, when Lou flashed a wicked smile, 'Well, guys, I've decided on a 'tree change.' I'm putting the house on the market and I'm moving to Coffs Harbour.' And then, in a more sombre voice, he added, 'I'll miss you both very much, but I think the time has come for me to move on.'

'What!!' Martin was the first to speak, followed almost immediately by Karen: 'Coffs Harbour!'

And together: 'When?'

It suddenly occurred to Karen why Lou had seemed restless over the last couple of weeks. 'And how did this come about?' she asked when she'd recovered her thoughts.

'Well, as you know, I've got several customers in Coffs Harbour, including the large resort a few kilometres north of the town. I've been calling on the resort for four or five years and have come to know the management there quite well. Two weeks ago, they offered me a job managing the front desk. I told them I don't have any direct experience in hospitality, but they reckon I've called on enough hotels and resorts over the years to know what makes a good front desk. You know, being attentive to guests, giving them what they want, understanding management's IT system. I reckon I can do that! So, I accepted the job yesterday. Plus, I think it's time I got off my butt and made a move to get on with the rest of my life.' He grinned broadly and topped up their drinks as he added: 'Besides which, you guys can come up and stay anytime you like, and I'll look after you.'

His smile faded slightly as he stared at them, wondering what they thought about his news. It was Karen who spoke first. 'Oh, Lou, it's a bit of a shock, but I'm so pleased for you. What an adventure! And good for you doing something positive with your life.'

Karen spoke from the heart; she was genuinely pleased for Lou. *This will open up his world,* she thought. *He'll meet new people...hopefully, even some female ones.* Much as Karen had been trying to help Lou meet ladies—via websites such as RSVP, parties, even one or two of her available friends—it hadn't worked. Nobody stood a chance when compared to Carole.

Lou smiled and reached over and squeezed Karen's hand in appreciation of her support.

Martin hesitated for a moment before he spoke. 'Well, I hope it works out for you, Lou—it's a big step to take for someone on their own. What'll you do if you don't like it there? Where will you live?' And then, as an afterthought, he added, 'Of course, we'll miss you very much.'

Martin couldn't quite let himself be one hundred percent positive for his friend. He found it difficult to hide his disappointment. He would be losing a friend. He liked Lou, and they had formed a comfortable, easy friendship. Martin hadn't had many of those throughout his life.

And so, six weeks later, with the house sold and everything packed, Lou drove north to take up a new life in Coffs Harbour.

8

A MOVE TO THE COUNTRY

Coffs Harbour is a picturesque regional city of about 70,000 people, on the coast of New South Wales, about a six-hour drive north of Sydney. It's known for its beautiful beaches, as well as the hinterland's lush green forests and banana plantations. It is the only place in New South Wales where the Great Dividing Range meets the Pacific Ocean, and whales are often spotted between June and November.

Karen and Martin visited Lou several times and, on each occasion, Lou drove them around the area and pointed out all the reasons he loved living in Coffs.

'You guys would fit right in here,' he'd said. 'Clean air, sunny days, not much traffic. There are even some good restaurants. It's the lifestyle you deserve after all the years you've both worked.'

So, it came as a shock to nobody when Karen and Martin decided to move to Coffs Harbour in 2013, when Martin retired at sixty-five. That had been five years ago, and they loved it as much now as they did then.

Karen had agreed to the move provided she could return to Sydney or Melbourne to visit friends and relatives, or to get away, anytime she wanted. This was non-negotiable. But Martin was so thrilled when she said she would move he would have agreed to anything.

The occasional need to get away on her own became stronger as time went by. While it was a comforting feeling to know Martin loved her, his love was often overwhelming in its intensity. Karen sometimes felt she was being smothered by Martin's crushing love. In his mind, they were joined at the hip, and Karen had to get away sometimes in order to reclaim her identity, her inner self.

As she pulled into the drive of the grand white two-storey house she and Martin had bought on their first house-hunting trip to Coffs Harbour, Karen smiled smugly to herself. They were living the good life, enjoying the fruits of their labour—well, mainly the fruits of Martin's labour—and life was almost everything she had imagined retirement would be. Nice big house in a good neighbourhood, good cars, the occasional overseas holiday, a comfortable existence.

It was Friday afternoon, which meant she would have the whole day to herself tomorrow when Martin played golf with his mates. He had always been involved in some form of sport. He was disappointed he had to give up tennis when his knees began to give him trouble before they left Sydney. He'd tried lawn bowls when they first came to Coffs, but it was no substitute for tennis, so these days, he concentrated on golf and played every Saturday. From what she could tell, he and his golfing partners seemed to spend a lot more time in the clubhouse after the game than they did playing golf. And then, of course, she got a hole-by-hole description of every stroke Martin had played when he got home. Karen didn't mind being bored rigid by tales of golf; after all, she got to enjoy a wonderful day of peace and solitude to herself every Saturday.

Martin was pottering about in the back garden as Karen drove into the garage and was sweeping up the Poinciana tree's fallen flowers in the centre of the lawn. He met her in the garage and carried the plants and bags of soil she'd bought to the garden shed, chattering away the whole time about anything and everything. Karen had learned many years ago how to switch off from Martin's steady stream of chatter, and so, although she could hear his voice, she wasn't listening.

They had stashed everything in the shed and were walking back inside when she interrupted him briefly to ask, 'Martin, I'm making a cup of tea. Would you like one?'

'I'd love a cup of your tea, thanks. You make terrific tea.'

She smiled as she filled the jug with water and switched it on, then took cups and tea bags from the cupboard. She caught Martin's eye and he smiled at her. Karen had been making cups of 'terrific tea' three or four times a day, every day, for the past thirty-six years. That's a lot of tea! It was a standing joke between them: 'Martin, would you like a cup of tea?' 'I'd love a cup of your tea, thanks. You make terrific tea.'

Always the same words, and it always made them smile.

They settled down on the comfy sofa in the living area with their tea, and he proceeded to tell her all about the weather heading their way in the next four to five days. Oh, how Martin loved talking about the weather and its intricacies. This was followed by a discourse on 'the stupid guy over the road who hasn't got any idea of how you use a leaf blower properly—what a mess he made of their garden,' followed by 'the idiot postman who squeezed a small parcel into our letterbox instead of delivering it to the door.'

It seemed Martin could find a problem with everybody he encountered. Perhaps that's what came from working for the Tax Office for forty-three years, even if he was extremely high up in the Office and earned big money.

Martin had started at the Tax Office at the bottom of the ladder and had gradually worked his way up to the 'almost' top. He had never been good at interacting with people, but he was a natural at working systemically and diligently on micro-understanding all the various aspects of the Tax Act. Nobody else came close to his understanding of the complicated and often ambiguous workings of the Tax Act. He was often sent to Canberra to explain complicated details regarding tax implications to various Chiefs of Treasury.

His career had suited his personality. He rarely had to engage with other employees, and the office had other staff more suited than him to deal with the public. He could often be undiplomatic, and although he was completely unaware of it, he sometimes made people feel uncomfortable in social situations when they found out he worked for the Tax Office—a bit like the sinking feeling you get in your stomach when the

Police Breathalyzer Unit pulls you over and you instantly regret having had that second drink with dinner.

As Karen drank her tea and appeared to be listening to Martin's every word, in her mind, she was going over the things she appreciated about him.

She had never been 'in love' with Martin and was aware of that when she married him. She had never felt a thrill when he touched her, or a rush of adrenalin when they made love, but over the years she had become very fond of him—he made her feel warm and wanted, and she was obviously the most important thing in his life. She loved the way he looked at her sometimes, still attracted to her after all these years. He often told her how much he loved her, and as far as she knew—and she knew him very well—he had never looked at another woman. Yes, he was self-centred and often abrasive, but he had some particularly good points too.

When they had first started going out together, she had been impressed by the way he dressed. He took pride in his appearance and wore his rather expensive clothes well. He was a tall man, six feet two when they met—more like six feet now—with mid-brown hair, a good tan, and strong facial features. She had always been proud to be seen out with him. The first time he took her to his apartment, Karen was astonished at how beautiful it was. And the view over the harbour took her breath away. Like Martin himself, everything looked good quality, polished, classy.

The first time she met Martin's elder brother, Tim, Karen liked him instantly. He was quite different from Martin. Not much to look at, but an endearing personality, natural and unaffected, and Karen and Tim developed a strong bond over the years. When she married Martin, Karen had been delighted to have Tim as a brother-in-law and would have loved it if Tim and Sue had lived closer. But she and Martin visited them in Melbourne every year, and Tim and Sue and their children drove up to Coffs for school holidays to stay with Karen and Martin, usually once a year.

Much to Karen's disappointment, they saw less of them when Tim was posted to Singapore to set up the new branch of the law firm. As a reward, Tim was made a partner. The two boys had chosen their careers well, and both reaped the benefits of hard work and commitment.

Early in their marriage, Karen learned Martin was an extraordinarily complex and sensitive person, and although she never had the chance to meet his parents, she thought they had a lot to answer for. In several conversations with Tim, she had gleaned a fair idea of the boys' upbringing by what seemed to be an often-absent father who didn't get involved in the boys' discipline when he was home, and a straitlaced, puritanical mother who, according to Tim, fawned over Martin and pandered to his every wish. He told her, with not a hint of rancour, that following a difficult birth when they nearly lost both mother and son, Martin became the golden-haired boy who could do no wrong. This probably explained why Martin always expected to get his own way. According to Tim, Martin got his short temper from their mother, who did not tolerate anyone who didn't play by her rules.

Martin's short temper was confirmed one day in Sydney before he retired. He was running late for work and driving too fast. He had cut another driver off while trying to change lanes. The other driver hadn't let him in quickly enough, and Martin completely lost it. He flew into a rage and deliberately drove into the other car, causing traffic chaos, and making him even later for work. Police were called and Martin was charged with dangerous driving. For many years, when Martin would retell the story, the driver of the other car was always in the wrong and driving dangerously. 'Drivers like him shouldn't be allowed on the roads!' he'd said.

It wasn't that Karen was frightened of Martin's temper; it was more a matter of keeping the peace. It had taken her several years to learn how to live with his temperament, his flare-ups, and his self-centredness, which had started with his birth. *Avoid poking the bear* was a line from a book she had read many years ago, and repeating the line in her head had staved off many an argument over the years.

Karen had the type of personality that could roll with the punches, and so she could handle Martin most of the time. She liked most people she met, and in her younger days had rarely let anyone upset her, although that seemed to be changing as she got older. She smiled and thought to herself, *I wonder what I'll be like at eighty—Mrs. Cranky Pants!*

'Martin, you haven't forgotten Lou's coming for dinner tonight, have you?' Karen took another biscuit off the plate between them and broke it in two, popping one half in her mouth as she spoke.

'No, I went to the fish market on the wharf and got some nice fresh Barramundi, which I'm going to do on the barbecue, with one or two of Nigella's fabulous salads, and the pavlova roll I made this afternoon for sweets.'

Martin had long been in love with Nigella Lawson—*wasn't every man in the English-speaking world?*—and had every recipe book she had ever produced. They could have lived for many years off the recipes in Martin's collection of Nigella's cookbooks.

Another thing Karen admired about Martin was that he was a superb cook. He made dinner four nights a week, and Karen looked forward to those nights. She would sit on one of the high timber and leather-upholstered stools at the white marble countertop, drinking a glass of wine watching him peel and chop, make a special sauce, grill a carefully prepared fish or piece of Wagyu, toss a salad of her favourite greens, all the while chatting about the day's events, the latest news, the shambolic state of politics in this country. He understood the detail in any recipe even if he didn't often use one, could produce a meal out of practically nothing in minutes if he had to, and could conjure up the most amazing sweets.

Karen openly and sincerely admired this ability and had always wished she were as capable in the kitchen; but it was not to be. Karen's forte was in handling people.

She was looking forward to Lou coming over for dinner tonight. He was a good friend, and he enjoyed coming to their place for dinner as much as he liked to reciprocate at his home. Tonight, they would have a lovely meal, a few drinks, and some good conversation.

Lou and Martin disagreed on several subjects, especially football, but Lou was such a diplomat their discussions never descended into nasty arguments. The three of them enjoyed these dinner conversations equally, but Karen often thought it was a shame Lou hadn't found a lady friend he could bring along.

Over the years, he had asked several women guests at the resort out for coffee, a few for dinner, but none had interested him enough to want to get to really know them. He had met one lady whom Karen thought might turn out to be 'the one'—she had even stayed over at his place on a few occasions—but Lou had simply let it slip away, not wanting her to become a permanent fixture in his life. Unfortunately, they all fell short when compared to Carole.

Finishing her tea, Karen put her cup and saucer on the kitchen counter. 'I've got something to show you,' she called, as she disappeared into her art room, reappearing with a small canvas in her hands.

'I finally finished the portrait of Lou and I'm going to give it to him tonight,' Karen said, as she turned the canvas around and proudly held the painting up for Martin's approval. She was quietly thrilled with it now it was finished.

Martin stood back and had a good look at the painting, which still smelled strongly of the varnish Karen had applied earlier in the day.

'That is really very good, Karen. You're so talented. I don't know why you don't do more with your paintings. You could sell a lot more if you wanted to.'

'Martin, you know how I feel about my painting—it's a hobby! I don't care what anyone else thinks of my paintings, I do them for the pleasure of getting it right, even if I only get it right about every tenth time! I enjoy the challenge. I don't care if I sell a painting or not. I'd rather give one to someone who likes it than hassle over price.' Then she smiled and added, 'But I am pleased with this one of Lou. I hope he likes it.'

Friday evening was a most enjoyable night: a wonderful meal, some great French champagne Lou had brought specially to celebrate it being Friday, and lots of laughs. Even the heavy discussion about the upcoming federal election ended with all three of them agreeing not one of the parties was worth voting for. Lou was a Labor supporter who believed in an egalitarian society; Martin was a Liberal voter who believed a Labor government couldn't handle finances, and when Labor was in government, the country's debt always skyrocketed. Karen was the original swing voter, and the way she felt about this election was she couldn't decide on the lesser of the two evils. The more champagne they drank, the more their views mellowed until they were almost on a par.

To make the evening perfect, Lou absolutely loved his painting. He was quiet for a minute as he took it in, then said, 'Karen, I can't tell you what this means to me. I'm only sorry Carole didn't get to see it. She would have loved it as much as I do.'

Lou had been on his own for several years now. Carole had been the love of his life, but he was never morose or self-pitying. Martin was concerned when Lou was silent for a minute or two, so he directed both him and Karen into the living room, insisting they all have another drink to toast the painting.

'A toast to 'Portrait of Lou' by the acclaimed artist, Karen Cosgrove, valued at one million dollars, but gifted to the sitter, Mr. Lou Bristow.'

Lou laughed as Karen took a bow.

As Karen and Lou sat comfortably in the big armchairs, Martin made coffee in the kitchen, tunelessly humming to himself all the while. He added the plate of tiny, filled, chocolate profiteroles he'd made in the morning to the tray holding the coffees and ceremoniously deposited it on the coffee table in the living room.

'Martin, you've done yourself proud,' said Lou, as he took a profiterole from the plate and popped it into his mouth. 'These are fabulous. Where'd you get the recipe?'

'Where do you think? Nigella, of course! Nobody does sweets like Nigella.'

'Oh God, don't ask him how he made them. We'll be here all night.' Karen rolled her eyes, then smiled. 'They are wonderful, Martin. They'd go very well with a brandy.'

'Brandies all round, then,' Martin announced, as he poured French brandy into three brandy balloons.

By midnight, all three were well on the way to being drunk and there was no way Karen was going to let Lou drive home, even if it was only a ten-minute drive. When she insisted he stay the night in the spare room, he gratefully accepted the offer.

She was tired and had had too much to drink, but it had been a most enjoyable four or five hours—fun, stimulating, never boring. Karen was happily married to Martin, who, for all his faults, was a good husband, but she had always enjoyed the company of other men. She had a great relationship with

Lou—he was a good friend and was always interesting and interested.

When she thought about it and looked back on her life, she had known and worked with several men who had impacted her life. Her boss at the advertising agency when she was in her early twenties had taught her about loyalty and hard work. A man she had worked with at the law firm had shown her that kindness and respect for others were the cornerstones of life. And from Martin, she had learned about herself, learned to understand her capabilities and shortcomings, learned how to adapt her mindset depending on the circumstances.

At fifty-eight, she was still trying to get it right, and nights like tonight were a reward for the trying.

As she prepared for bed while Martin stacked the dishwasher and put the garbage out, Karen thought how glad she was she and Martin no longer bothered with sex. She would not have been up for it tonight.

From day one, sex between Karen and Martin had never been exciting, and the initial feelings of lust early in their marriage had quickly faded, replaced by a comfortable intimacy. Fortunately, their sexual appetites were similar, and it suited them both not to have to think about sex often.

Years ago, their situation reached the stage where they didn't even bother with contraception. The odds of their conceiving were extremely low, so it came as quite a shock when Karen fell pregnant with Tony, their only child. Karen's morning sickness lasted all through the pregnancy, and it was a difficult birth.

Martin was the proudest father she had ever known. He was captivated by Tony, couldn't get enough of him. He would nurse him, change him, walk him to the park in the pram, stopping to talk to anyone who would listen, regaling them with minute details of his unique and extraordinary baby. But Tony was a colicky baby, and Karen could never get a full night's sleep during the first year before he settled down. It took her about eighteen months to get into a baby routine, during which time, sex became even less frequent. Martin was so besotted with his son it didn't bother him when Karen's desire for sex faded away.

Karen couldn't remember the last time they had sex, but one thing was definite: she knew it was the very last thing she felt like tonight as she slipped between the clean smooth sheets and fell asleep instantly.

9

A NEW HOBBY?

Karen shuddered at the thought of what Martin was going to go through in the next few hours as she drove him to his dentist appointment at ten-thirty. The two wisdom teeth had been giving him trouble for a few years and were at long last being removed. Their dentist in Coffs Harbour had suggested he probably wouldn't feel like driving home. She had always hated going to the dentist and the thought of having teeth removed made her feel slightly sick. Poor Martin. She'd cook him something special for dinner—maybe some soup, followed by his favourite ice cream.

Knowing she had a couple of hours free, Karen drove home and made herself a cup of tea. She hoisted herself up on a barstool and sat at the long marble countertop in the kitchen. She took a sip of her tea and opened the paper. It was a great place to spread out the *Sydney Morning Herald*, a large broadsheet newspaper which Martin collected every morning from the newsagent.

She liked to start at the front page of the paper and read every section. She turned a page and was about halfway through, when a thought occurred: *Ooh, I've got some chocolate biscuits in the pantry. Think I'll have one with my cuppa.* As she hopped down off the stool to go to the pantry, one of the articles on the page she had just turned caught her eye—it was about various websites and their addresses. She glanced over the article but stopped abruptly when a web address on the page triggered something in her mind, transporting her back to her youth. The web address was www.letsbefriends.com .

That looks like one of those pen pal things I used to do as a kid, thought Karen. *I must check it out later and see if I can find someone interesting to correspond with.*

She'd always been an excellent correspondent. When she was about nine years old, she had filled in a form in the children's section of the Sunday paper. They were asking boys and girls who were interested in writing to someone with similar interests to supply their details and a pen pal would contact them. A week later, she'd received a few replies from girls around her age who had also filled in the form.

She began corresponding with two of the girls: Elizabeth in Perth, Western Australia, and Marlene in Cairns, Queensland. Although she didn't ever get to meet either of the girls, she'd continued to exchange letters with Elizabeth for seven or eight years until Elizabeth met a boy, after which she lost interest in writing to a girl on the other side of the country since, apparently, boys in Perth were suddenly much more interesting. Karen had enjoyed corresponding with girls who nobody in her school, or at home, knew.

Karen scribbled the web address on a slip of paper and tucked it into her shopping notepad in the pantry as she picked up the packet of biscuits. And promptly forgot about it.

A couple of days later, she came across the piece of paper in the pantry. Martin was at his book club meeting/lunch and she had some spare time for herself. *A good time to go and check out that website.*

The website was a bit confusing, not user-friendly at all. The home page was full of small-size text. She scanned through it quickly—too boring to read—and worked out they wanted a profile and an email address. Karen had always been very wary of putting anything about herself on the internet, and she certainly wasn't going to put a photo on the site. Instead, she used the name and email address she employed when she wrote letters to the Editor, another hobby of hers. No one else knew this name or email address, and she felt safer, more anonymous, when using the internet. She added a very generic profile, but listed her interests as politics, sport, reading, and people.

She didn't think she'd mention this to Martin—no need for him to know anything about it. It could be her little hobby conducted completely without his interference or well-meaning, but patronizing, advice.

On her profile, she stated she lived in Victoria as she didn't want to connect with anyone who might be from the area or who may know her, and put her age down as fifty, hoping to correspond with someone younger. She found the opinions of younger people interesting, even if she didn't always agree with them.

Over the next few days, Karen received a few replies, some of which were from people living on the other side of the world, which she thought was particularly interesting. However, after reading them more thoroughly, she realised they were all from men. She was surprised; she had been expecting to hear from other women. She rummaged through the drawer where they kept old newspapers for wrapping rubbish in to see if the newspaper was still there. She managed to find most of it in the drawer, including the page she was looking for, and read the article in detail. It seemed she had misunderstood it. The article was about misleading website addresses and how web addresses can sometimes relate to completely different things than what is suggested in the address.

She logged onto the site again, but this time, she read every word. When she had originally scanned the article in the paper, she had completely missed the bit about 'Let's Be Friends' being an adult site. On checking the site again, she saw where she had unknowingly checked the box next to 'Men.' She also discovered the site forwarded on names of those men who were interested in her profile and wanted to contact her.

Her inner voice silently screamed, *Do nothing! Do nothing for a week.*

Over the next few days, Karen found herself thinking about the replies she had received. In the back of her mind, her interest was piqued, and the more she thought about the emails, the more she felt a little tingle of excitement. She didn't want to meet anyone but thought it might be fun to reply to a few. In her profile, she had said her interests were reading, sport, people, and politics—who knows, there could be a couple of men out there who could conduct an interesting correspondence on any of these topics. She felt quite safe as they were all situated a long way away from Coffs Harbour, and these men didn't know her real name, anyway.

A week later, when the opportunity arose, Karen reread the emails. And deleted all except three, which were a cut above the rest—courteous, well written, and included no photos.

Paul, fifty-three, lived in Victoria, married with one son. He was married and intended to stay married but was seeking some stimulation and excitement in his life. His email was gentle and non-threatening, and he stated how he would very much like to correspond with Karen. Given his situation—married and not looking to leave—Karen considered him a very low-risk 'extra man' in her life.

Jeff, sixty-eight, Australian-born living in France, was retired, widowed, with one daughter who lived nearby and one married son who lived in Sydney. He had been married for many years, but since his wife died five years ago, his interest in life had diminished. A friend sent him a link to the website and suggested it might be a good way to get some spark back into his life.

His reply was beautifully written, expressive, interesting, confident but gentle, and in it he mentioned he sometimes travelled to Sydney to visit his son. Karen considered him a low risk 'extra man' in her life as well, since he lived a long way away and seemed to be every bit the gentleman.

Chris, seventy, from Colorado in the US, was retired and married for the fourth time to a possessive woman. He had six kids all over the country. His reply was gracious and courteous, beautifully written if tentative, and stated he would be absolutely delighted to correspond with Karen. He seemed low risk, especially as he lived on the other side of the world.

Karen replied to Jeff, then Chris, and eventually to Paul. And three interesting relationships began.

Jeff and Karen became genuine 'pen pals,' exchanging photos and many frank and heart-warming emails over the following months. Jeff was a wonderful letter-writer, sometimes writing a long and interesting, sometimes rambling, letter, sometimes a short, funny one-liner, and Karen looked forward to his emails. It was a wonderful way to develop a genuine online friendship, writing things in a letter you wouldn't necessarily say to a person face-to-face. Very eighteenth-century!

Jeff told her he had lived in London for twenty years working as a government advisor before retiring a few years ago. Karen thought him an intelligent man, and they shared many complex and interesting discussions over the internet about several deep and world-affecting issues. Judging from the photos he sent her, it looked like he had a beautiful garden, which he kept in immaculate condition. Karen also loved her garden and they often exchanged hints and advice about plants and flowers; interesting information, as they lived in different hemispheres where the seasons were opposite.

Jeff was interested in politics, especially European, which Karen found eminently more interesting than what was happening in Australia. Martin had always considered himself a font of knowledge about world politics, but after hearing from someone who lived in Europe and had their ear to the ground—and was obviously no fool about such things—Karen realised she would have to be careful not to contradict Martin and his opinions when she knew he was not quite correct. Thanks to Jeff, she learned another perspective on world events, other than what was on the news on TV or in the Australian papers. He had a good mind and an all-encompassing worldview.

When Karen had listed her interests as sport on her profile for the website, in her mind she had been referring to tennis and netball, plus she loved the gymnastics when the Olympic Games were on. However, Jeff's twenty years living in the UK had imbued him with a love of cricket, a sport which left Karen cold. He would occasionally go on about a match being played between the UK and Australia, presuming since she lived in Australia, she would automatically be interested in cricket. He seemed to enjoy telling her all about it, often quoting scores and players' names, and she never mentioned she was not the least bit interested in the game. Martin had always been a cricket fan and sometimes went down to Sydney for certain matches. She smiled to herself when she thought Martin and Jeff would probably have become good friends had they known each other. They would have had many conversations, or even arguments, about cricket.

Jeff was too much of a gentleman to mention the subject of sex too soon. But once he broke the ice, six months into their correspondence, he wrote some wonderfully sexy stuff using rather old-fashioned language, and the correspondence from him was often like something out of an Emily Brontë novel. He was a very romantic, gentle soul; a caring, loving man.

Karen continued to correspond with Jeff, presuming she would never meet him, and enjoyed having him as a 'pen pal.' However, as time went by, she sensed her relationship with Jeff, even though it was at this innocent stage, could become a problem. He was becoming extremely fond of her and told her more than once how much her letters meant to him. She became worried it could get out of hand, especially since he lived alone, and the relationship had become a big part of his day-to-day life.

Probably best to tell a white lie, Karen thought, as she sat at her computer one rainy day composing her email to him, telling him they must stop writing to each other. The reason she offered was that, unfortunately, her husband had become suspicious, and under the circumstances, she could not risk any further communication. She hoped he could understand the predicament she was in and the distress it had caused her. He wrote back immediately, devastated to know this was the end, but he understood her situation and did not want to cause any trouble in her marriage. He wished her well and told her, no matter what might happen in the future, he would always be there for her, and he loved her and that would never change.

Chris turned out to be a slightly riskier acquaintance. In his second or third email, he told her he was a Vietnam veteran and suffered from PTSD, had bouts of depression from time to time, was slightly erratic, and saw a psychiatrist regularly, as did many Vietnam vets. He said his wife controlled his life following his nervous breakdown ten years earlier, and he resented her control but could not do anything about it. Karen suspected he subconsciously needed somebody else to take charge of his day-to-day life but, at the same time, deeply resented that control.

Karen thought he would be extremely hard to live with, a bit of a loose cannon, a person who needed constant praise. However, he had a great sense of humour and could be very funny in some of his emails. She would sometimes laugh out loud as she read an email from him, but occasionally, his emails were very dark, and she thought he probably had suicidal thoughts from time to time.

Even though he was American, and the US had played a different part in the Vietnam War than Australia, Karen felt a connection with Chris. She had read many accounts of the effects the Vietnam War had on the young men who returned from the battlefield vastly different people.

There were so many men around the country suffering PTSD as a result of a war nobody believed in at the time, and who had been ignored by virtually the rest of Australia when they returned home. As those men had grown older, a lot of them had banded together to support each other and become a voice in the community. As if fighting in a war they knew little about in truly dreadful conditions weren't bad enough, the insult and confusion of being rejected when they returned home changed many lives forever.

The situation hadn't been much different for American vets when they returned home, and apparently, Chris's first marriage had broken down within four months of his return from Vietnam.

Karen continued to correspond with Chris and found some of his war memories very moving. He lived so far away, their relationship seemed harmless enough, and he constantly told her how much he enjoyed her emails. On a good day, he was a great correspondent. Some of his emails were hilarious; some were quite poetic.

He related his life story one email at a time. Born the youngest of seven kids, on a remote farm in the mountains of western Montana, he never had a chance to know his father, who took off, never to be heard of again, when Chris was six months old. His mother struggled on, managing to feed and clothe him and his four brothers and two sisters until Chris started school. She passed away when he was five, and all the kids were farmed out to different foster homes. He never saw any of them again.

He ended up with a family in Idaho, beaten by his foster father and continually screamed at by his foster mother until he joined the army at age seventeen, when he lied about his age. He enjoyed army life; he didn't have to think for himself, and the discipline straightened him out a bit. The army taught him how to be a soldier, but he'd been through the school of hard knocks, and the damage done to him both physically and emotionally in his childhood set him up for a troubled life.

He had continued to serve for twenty years but had left when he met and married his current, and fourth, wife. Like many men who have been in the military, he did not handle civilian life well, and the adjustment he was required to make, combined with his Vietnam experiences, caused him to become depressed and he was diagnosed with PTSD. He was happiest, he told Karen, when he was with his Vietnam mates, when he'd organised meetups with as many of them as possible a few times a year.

Their correspondence continued for a few months until Chris wrote that he was planning on coming to Australia for a holiday, alone, and would love to meet Karen. It took her three days to compose her reply. She didn't want to hurt him unnecessarily, but she had to make it very clear she would not agree to meet him. Had she been leading him on all this time? Would he turn nasty?

On the third day, she replied. Her email was clear and concise, gentle but unequivocal—there was no room for ambiguity. She said although she would possibly enjoy meeting him, she didn't think it was a good idea and made it very clear it was not going to happen.

He replied immediately and thanked her for her honesty and straightforwardness—something he'd heard was an Australian trait—but he was also disappointed. His emails dropped off considerably after that and eventually, they ceased altogether. Karen was sorry to see him go but was also relieved when their correspondence stopped.

On reflection, after rereading all the original replies she had received, Karen wondered what motivated these men to want to establish a relationship of some kind with a woman over the internet, often half a world away. They sounded lonely, yet most of them were married.

Why had the men lost the feeling of reciprocal love and togetherness they had in the early days of their marriages? Quite a few of the emails Karen had received mentioned lost intimacy with their wives, wives who had drifted away into their own lives and lost interest in them as partners, wives who took them for granted.

What had caused that to happen? Whose fault was it? Were the men not as caring as they once were? Did the women neglect the men when babies came along, and if so, did that neglect become a habit?

Judging from the first batch of replies, these men did not want to leave their wives; they wanted to feel some sort of intimacy in their lives, a connection with another female. Of course, some of them wanted extramarital sex, but she was sure a lot of them just wanted someone to listen to them, to take notice of them, to appreciate them.

And then there was Paul.

10

PAUL'S STORY—Part One

From an early age, Paul knew he was different from the other kids. He didn't talk much, often giving one-word answers when asked questions by teachers and classmates. The other kids would get together and play in groups during breaks, but he wasn't included in their games—and he didn't make friends easily, but then, he didn't want to become involved with them and their childish activities, anyway. During the breaks, he could usually be found sitting on a seat in the playground reading on his own. But that didn't mean he felt lonely. It was his choice. He liked to be on his own; he liked to put distance between himself and other people. It gave him time to think and observe what was going on around him. At social events, having to engage with adults stressed him out, and his subconscious sense of superiority over other kids meant he tended to ignore them. He lived in his own world and was happy there.

He was a very bright student who enjoyed concentrating on his studies. His favourite thing was puzzles—at the age of seven, he could complete the Rubik's Cube in minutes—but he also loved arithmetic, and was always at the top of his math class.

When he started primary school, Paul quickly worked out he was good at two things: anything to do with numbers, and running. He loved running, and even though he enjoyed most sports, he was better at running, primarily because it was a solitary endeavour. Sports and Athletics Day was always a good day for Paul, who invariably won any race he entered. The farther he ran, the better he felt. It invigorated him, and he knew he could win comfortably over the other kids at Sports Day races, which only increased his feeling of superiority.

'And how was Sports Day today, Paul?' his mother asked, as she passed his fully laden plate back to him at the dinner table.

'Good,' replied Paul. The one-word answer.

'Did you win any races?' asked his dad. Drawing information out of Paul was like trout fishing—a slow process, but usually worthwhile in the end.

'Yes. Heats, and finals of four races.'

'Good on you, Paul. Well done. You seem to really enjoy running.' Hi father smiled proudly at him. 'What do you think about getting some training to help you pace yourself? You seem to like the longer distances.'

His mother smiled kindly at him as she reached over and put her hand on his arm. 'Your father and I have discussed it, and we think it would be a good idea. You obviously have a talent for running, but it often helps if you're taught the correct way of doing something you love, whatever it is.'

Carefully placing his knife and fork on either side of his plate, Paul thought for a moment, weighing up if he thought it would be beneficial. 'All right. If you think it's a good idea.' And then, because he had never actually said it before, he grinned and added, 'I like running more than anything.'

A trainer was found, and Paul's running moved up a notch. Mr. Walker, the trainer, could see real potential in Paul. Mr. Walker shared insights on pacing and technique, drawing from his years of experience as a competitive runner. But Paul was a troublesome child to coach—the kid seemed to know instinctively what to do, how to pace himself, when to conserve energy and when to put in extra effort.

Paul persevered with Mr. Walker for a few years, mainly to appease his parents, but he didn't learn much from him. The regimen of the training sessions bored Paul; he loved to run. When he ran on the weekends, just for the fun of it, he could run farther and more comfortably than when Mr. Walker was watching him, telling him what to do and when.

When he was thirteen and in his third year of training, Paul initiated a conversation with his parents one evening at the dinner table. Mr. and Mrs. McElhone glanced at each other in surprise—Paul so rarely spoke before being spoken to.

'I've had enough of Mr. Walker telling me what to do. Can you cancel him? I prefer to run on my own. The longer the distance, the better.'

Mr. Walker was disappointed when they told him. He thought Paul had real potential and wished him well at their last session. He also suggested Paul enter the Melbourne half-marathon if he wanted to test himself against other distance runners.

Cross-country running, at his own pace, was what Paul enjoyed the most. By about the third mile, he could feel the muscles in his legs beginning to burn, then he would take a deep breath and break through the burn barrier, powering ahead with renewed energy. It didn't take long after that sensation kicked in for him to find his rhythm and settle into a stride for as long as he wanted to run. The sense of freedom, of clearing his head of all thought, of putting one foot down after the other, was exhilarating. He could run for hours, his spirits rising with each step, the wind in his face, the sun on his back.

He was fifteen when he ran his first half-marathon in the Melbourne Festival and came in thirty-second place. He was just getting into his stride when the race finished. After regularly running longer and longer distances over the next twelve months, he ran the full marathon at the same event the following year and finished fifteenth. That was more like it, but he knew he could do better. By the time he was nineteen, and after having run the marathon each year, he was very pleased with himself when he finished fifth!

The final exams at high school were not difficult for Paul, so it was no surprise when he topped the school in every subject and achieved a Tertiary Entrance Ranking of 99.8 percent.

He was eighteen years old and didn't know what he wanted to do with his life. His years at school had given his life purpose—a routine, a rhythm—but ever since school had finished, that purpose had disappeared, and he felt a bit lost. He didn't know what to do with himself other than run. As much as he thought about it, tried to analyse his feelings about the future, he didn't seem to be able to decide what he wanted to do as far as a career went. His mother and father were keen for him to do Medicine or Dentistry but neither profession interested him. Math had always been straightforward and uncomplicated for him at school, so he took the easy way out and enrolled in Science and Mathematics at the University of Melbourne. He figured that would give him a couple of years to work out what he really wanted to do.

A few months later, as chance would have it, Paul found himself sitting next to the same guy at several lectures. After this happened three or four times and the other fellow had still not spoken to him other than to nod hello, Paul sensed a kindred spirit and introduced himself. He leaned a bit closer to the other boy and extended his hand. 'Hi, I'm Paul McElhone.'

The young man turned slightly towards Paul, somewhat surprised. 'Oh. Hi. I'm Tom Watson.' They shook hands as the lecturer entered the hall and the room fell silent, except for the shuffling of papers and books.

Once the lecture was over, students began packing up, chatting amongst themselves, some forming into groups as they drifted out of the lecture room. It had been the last lecture of the day, and the sound of the collective sigh of relief was audible.

Tom looked over at Paul, who was sitting quietly, desk cleared, bag packed. He seemed to be staring into space, thinking.

'Did you get all that?' Tom asked. 'You hardly seemed to make any notes.'

'Yeah. I thought it was straightforward. Made sense to me.' Paul turned his head towards Tom and frowned. 'Until he did the last calculation on the board. I don't reckon it was correct. What did you think of it?'

Tom looked downcast as he stuffed his notes into his battered briefcase. 'He'd lost me long before then.' Then, after a slight hesitation, he said, 'Um, would you like to get a drink at the Prince Alfred? You could explain your version of the calculation.'

Beers in hand, they found a seat at a small table in the pub and Paul explained what was wrong with the calculation. Tom nodded, but it was obvious he didn't really get it.

Tom explained, 'It's times like this when I wonder why I ever took Science and Mathematics. I'm more of a practical, hands-on sort of guy, but I dithered about for so long trying to decide what to do, this course was the only one with a couple of vacancies left.'

'I had trouble working out what to do with my life once high school was over. My dad tried to convince me it wasn't necessary to plan my entire future at this point in time. He said it didn't really matter what subjects I took in the first year; it would work itself out over time, and it would eventually become clear to me where my future lay.'

However, one thing he did know, and which he kept to himself, was he very much doubted Paul was correct about the calculation. He was sure the lecturer knew more about calculus than Paul did.

They continued to discuss the course and the lecturers. On their third beer, Paul placed his glass on the table and said, 'I believe I detect an American accent there. What part of the States are you from?

'I was born and raised in California. My dad is an executive with Hewlett-Packard, the computer company. He was transferred to Sydney three years ago, so I finished my high school education in Sydney. Then he was transferred to Melbourne late last year. I intend to go back to Palo Alto when I've finished uni here and do something in IT—programming or hardware; I haven't decided yet. How about you? What are you going to do?'

Paul thought about this for a moment. He wasn't good at answering questions quickly—he liked to think before he spoke. His mind ticked over while he formed his replied in his head before he said, 'I don't really know. I enrolled in Science and Maths because I don't have to study too hard and to give myself time to work out what I want to do. My parents would like me to do Medicine or Dentistry, but neither of them is for me. I'm hoping to come across something that lights my fire while I'm here at uni.'

A little later, after another pause in the conversation, and on their fourth beer, Paul said, 'We've got the afternoon off tomorrow; think I'll go for a run. Do you run?'

'God no!' Tom exclaimed in horror. 'I'm not into sport.'

Tom was tall and thin and wore the same black sweater and black jeans to uni every day. He had a pasty pallor and thick black eyebrows and his longish black hair was always dishevelled. He was good looking in a dark and brooding sort of way—always looked like he needed a shave yet, somehow, he managed to look elegant. Perhaps it was the long much-used scarf he always wore, casually draped around his neck as if he'd grabbed it and thrown it on as he rushed out the door on his way to uni. Or maybe it was the many rings on his long, slender fingers.

'So, what do you do, then?' Paul asked, grinning at Tom's reply.

'I play guitar. And keyboard. And drums. I'm quite good.'

'I'm quite good at running!' said Paul, and they both smiled and clinked glasses.

Tom went to the bar and returned with their fifth beers. Neither boy was good at conversation, but by this time, the beers had loosened them up and the words flowed more easily.

'You got a girlfriend?' asked Tom tentatively.

'No.' Paul paused. 'Don't get me wrong, I like girls, but they scare me a bit. You never know what they're thinking, what they want you to do or say. I'm not much of a talker, and I get tongue tied when I try and chat up a female. I end up feeling like an idiot. Easier not to even try. How about you?'

'Not at the moment. Used to, but she dumped me for the bass player. I play guitar with a couple of guys. We've played a few gigs at pubs around town and there are always plenty of eager girls there, so I guess I'll find another one sooner or later.'

'Let me know where you're playing next time. I like pub bands,' said Paul.

More silence, followed by more small talk, then eventually Paul stood and picked up his briefcase. 'I think I'll call it a night and get the train home.'

Tom collected his things, and as the two boys left the hotel, they shook hands and agreed to meet for a drink again soon.

They were similar in many ways—both introverts who enjoyed their own company, each trying to work out their place in the world and discover where they fitted in the grand scheme of things. One thing was certain—neither one would be joining the debating team anytime soon.

At the following week's lecture on calculus, and early in the lecture, the professor made an announcement: 'Oh, by the way, one of the figures in one of the calculations last week was incorrect. This is what it should have read,' and he proceeded to write up the corrected calculation on the board. Exactly as Paul had said it should be.

Tom glanced at Paul in wonder and thought to himself: *Hmmm, I may have underestimated this guy.*

Tom and Paul often found themselves in the bar of the Prince Alfred after the last lecture of the day, sitting at the tiny table in the corner, beer in hand. Both had taken English as an extra subject in the Bachelor of Science degree course. Tom was particularly good at and enjoyed English, but it didn't come easily to Paul—math was his thing. They often helped each other with notes and homework, and although Paul was a natural at numbers, Tom was a whiz on the computer. He owned a Commodore 64 and seemed to know everything about it—from what the software was capable of to how the hardware worked. He had even taken the computer apart and put it back together again several times, and it still worked! He was happy to share this knowledge with Paul. It was the mid-1980s and both boys realised computers were the future, and to know and understand how they did their magic was going to be the key to their success.

Paul went along to a couple of gigs where Tom's band played and enjoyed listening to them. He was amazed at the girls who literally threw themselves at Tom and the other guys. Tom could have had any one of them. They were certainly full on, scary, with their overt adoration and not-so-subtle sexual advances, but you wouldn't want to get tied up with one of them, no matter how appealing they looked. They reminded him of vultures fighting over carrion.

The first year at uni ended, and before they knew it, Tom and Paul had settled into the routine of the second year. Paul still lived at home with his parents and Tom with his father—his mother had died when he was eight, and his paternal grandmother had moved into their home in Palo Alto, California, and helped raise him. He missed her very much, particularly knowing she was so far away, and he and his dad had gone home for a few weeks over the Christmas break.

The second year became the third year, and suddenly, they were in the fourth year and coming to the end of their time at uni. Over the previous four years, Paul had had two girlfriends, albeit both short-lived relationships, while Tom had had at least twelve—sometimes seeing two girls at the same time, which, in Paul's opinion, was playing an extremely dangerous game. Each of Paul's girlfriends had been Tom's castoffs. He had still never managed to initiate a connection with a female, still felt intimidated by them, still felt foolish trying to start a conversation. At least with running, you weren't trying to impress anyone, just being true to yourself. But he felt comfortable with Tom. They had developed a good friendship with no pressure, no expectations. Similar in nature—except Tom was a chick magnet!

Exams would be happening soon, which hopefully, would result in both boys obtaining their degrees. One late September afternoon at the Prince Alfred, Tom returned to the table with their fourth beers as Paul organised some space on the table amongst the empty glasses. Tom sat down and took a sip of his beer.

'Dad and I are going back to Palo Alto for a couple of weeks when exams have finished. Why don't you come with us? You can stay with Gran and me—all you need is your airfare and some spending money. You'd love my grandma; she's a terrific woman, and she'd love you. Well, she'd love any friend of mine so no need to think you're anything special.' Tom laughed and punched Paul on the arm. 'The break would do you good, you know it would. And you could run some new trails—but don't expect me to run with you!'

Paul thought about this for a moment. The break would do him good and the thought of running somewhere new was certainly enticing, plus he'd never been invited anywhere before and he felt inwardly chuffed. He'd never been out of the country, and from what Tom had told him, California sounded interesting.

And it was. A whole new world opened up to Paul in California. It was big, it was brash, there seemed to be so much more of everything—people, shops, restaurants, life! And Tom was right about one thing—Paul loved Gran. What a fascinating lady. She'd been practically everywhere and done just about everything. She was funny, strong, hard as nails and sentimental at the same time, and full of the joy of life.

They'd been in California for a couple of weeks when they found out they had both passed their finals and were now faced with the big decision: what to do with the rest of their lives? When Tom's Aunt Lola in Arizona heard about his results, she invited both boys to come and stay with her for a couple of weeks to celebrate. She would cover the cost of everything—how could they refuse?

Tom had been to stay with Lola many times, and he loved how you never knew what would happen from one moment to the next when you were with her. He loved his eccentric aunt and loved staying with her. Lola was his mother's twin sister and had been the first person to comfort Tom and his father when his mum died. She had been distraught when Ellen died, but she had stayed with Tom and his dad and held things together during those terrible first few weeks, until his dad's mother had moved in permanently.

Arizona was another eye-opener for Paul, so different from California—a scorching desert of a place, dry and flat but full of fascinating colours and vegetation

They flew into Phoenix and caught the bus to Scottsdale, where Lola lived. As they approached her house, she came running down the front steps laughing and shouting her elation at the arrival of the two handsome young men who would be hers to care for and show off for the next two weeks. First Tom, and then Paul, each loving the huge warm hugs and many kisses Lola bestowed on them. She laughed and talked nonstop as she linked her arms through theirs, and the three of them climbed the steps as one. Paul was secretly thrilled by the way Lola took to him, as if she'd known him all his life.

Life with Lola was multicoloured and stereophonic. Paul was fascinated by her. She dressed like a gypsy, her flaming red hair tied up in a wildly bright scarf on the top of her head. The scarf had little bells on it that tinkled when she moved. Her long floaty skirt swished about her when she walked, revealing red suede high-heeled boots. She was flamboyant, outspoken, and her laugh was like a temple bell, loud and resonant.

She took both boys downtown to some of the many art galleries in Scottsdale several times. Everywhere they went, people knew her, their day made brighter by an encounter with Lola trailing the two young men. Paul had never been interested in art before, but after a few visits to the galleries with Lola, he began to learn to appreciate it.

They ate a huge variety of food at a huge variety of places, from sophisticated restaurants to tiny bars to take-out places that defied description. And drank many beers, including the Desert Rose made from cactus fruit, which also defied description.

The three of them went hot-air ballooning over the desert surrounding Phoenix during the full moon. It was spectacular.

It all seemed a million miles away from Melbourne, and Paul enjoyed himself as never before.

One of the reasons Lola could afford to do all these wonderful things was due to the success of her business. Several years ago, she had begun making weird and wonderful greeting cards, ostensibly for fun, but when serious orders began to roll in, she registered the business name 'Custom-Made Cards,' and, using the latest technology, including computers and colour printers, turned it into a moneymaking powerhouse. Her office was only a ten-minute drive from her home, and she had been shrewd enough in the early days to employ a dynamic, loyal manager to run the day-to-day business for her so she could wine and dine customers, and subsequently create more business.

During the second week of their stay, Lola had to deliver an order of special handmade name cards for an event at Taliesin West, Frank Lloyd Wright's winter home in the desert, a short drive out of town.

'Tomorrow morning, early, I'm driving out to Taliesin West to deliver some cards. Would you both like to come with me? It's a magnificent place and I'm sure you'll find it interesting. We need to get there well before the public arrives.'

Although Tom had heard of it, he had never been there. Paul had never even heard of it, but if Lola thought it was 'magnificent,' then it would probably be interesting at the very least.

It was a chilly morning, but the sun shone brilliantly in the azure sky, signalling the hot dry day to follow. They drove out into the desert, Lola at the wheel of her Cadillac convertible, the two boys in the back, grinning and punching each other like two little kids embarking on a big adventure. They passed huge buttes set against the distant purple mountains and at least a million cacti standing proudly in the red desert earth. It was like driving through a Disney movie. Lola parked the car in the staff parking area, and they walked up a small hill to the top of the rise. Taliesin West lay before them like a giant serpent basking in the early morning sunshine.

They stopped for a moment to admire the view, and Paul felt something stir deep inside him. The building looked like it had grown out of the desert and had settled comfortably into the surroundings to enjoy a very long life. The planes, the angles, the colours, all bathed in the morning glow of the sun, gave it a majesty and grandeur that took his breath away. Lola was right—it was a magnificent building, like nothing Paul had ever seen before. Unique, low-level, sprawling, peaceful. At one with the earth. A forever place.

'Wow, it's some building, isn't it, Paul?' Tom spoke quietly, not wanting to break the spell of the moment.

'Yes.' was all Paul could say.

'Well, come on, boys. Let's go have a closer look. I arranged for one of the tour guides to take you around before the public tours start at nine a.m. That gives you a good hour to have a look around.'

An hour? thought Paul. *I want to spend a week here!*

The next hour was a life-changing experience for Paul. It was then he realised what he wanted to do with his life. He wanted to design and create buildings that affected people the way Taliesin West had affected him.

He was quiet in the car on the way back as Tom and Lola chatted about the place and Lola told them a little about Frank Lloyd Wright and his place in American architecture. When he at last spoke, Paul told them he needed to go back there for the day tomorrow and asked Lola if he could borrow the car.

Tom turned and looked at Paul in astonishment. 'All day?! Whatever for?'

'I want to find out everything there is to know about Taliesin West and Frank Lloyd Wright.'

The holiday over, Paul hugged Gran goodbye and thanked her for the best holiday he'd ever had. He would love to have spent a few more weeks with them, and both Tom and Gran had begged him to stay, but he wanted to get back and find out more about studying Architecture at uni—how long would it take to qualify? Where was the best uni to do it? Could he get practical experience while studying?

It was quiet in the car as Tom drove him to the airport, both boys mentally pondering their futures. Paul finally spoke: 'So, you think you'll join Hewlett-Packard here and stake your future in computers? Should be easy—you know practically everything there is to know about them now! What'll it be—hardware or software?'

'Whichever one leaves me enough time for my music.' Tom replied, laughing. 'Seriously, I know I'll never make a lot of money from my music, but I also know both software and hardware are going to be **big** in the future, and I intend to be well prepared when that happens. So, the answer to your question is both! And compared to what the future holds for computers, I know nothing! Anyway, I've really enjoyed knowing you, man. We shouldn't let our friendship peter out because we live in different countries. Stay in touch; I mean it.'

Paul hesitated a moment before he spoke. 'That's why they invented email!' He looked away quickly, embarrassed his retort sounded flippant. He wanted to say so much more, but he couldn't manage it. Such is the lot of the introvert.

At the end of his first year studying Architecture, Paul secured a part-time job with a small group of architects in Melbourne—Glenwall, Green, and Associates—doing building applications, filing, measuring; they even allowed him to draw up some very basic plans. By the end of the year, he was sure there was a better way to do some of the basic stuff using a computer instead of a set square and ruler, so he enrolled in Computer Science and applied himself to both courses concurrently. He was a natural at Computer Science and took to it like a mouse to cheese.

Over the following year, he designed and wrote a basic software program, which enabled his bosses to draw some of the plans on a computer. An expensive and well-developed software program had been on the market for some time, but his was simple and cheap, and his bosses were delighted with his efforts.

Tom and Paul had maintained their friendship via email, and Paul didn't need twice asking when Tom suggested he come over to California for Christmas. It was great to catch up in person. By this time, Tom had formed a band and they played several gigs while Paul was staying with Tom and his grandma. On other nights, the boys stayed up late, drinking many beers and comparing notes on their careers and study. Paul showed Tom the software program he had written and explained it in detail. Tom was extremely impressed and between them they tweaked it here and there and made it more streamlined.

Once he qualified as an architect, the company offered Paul a permanent position, which he readily accepted. Working in the office all day, five days a week, Paul began to learn more about the running of the business—there was so much more to it than designing and drawing plans. Budgeting, as well as calculating the quantity of the various materials necessary for a building and their costs, was a nightmare, and extremely time-consuming. And then there was the problem of billing the clients, ensuring the company was making a profit at the end of the day.

Paul realised he needed to get back to the computer and work on a program that incorporated the design principles of architecture with the practical side of the business, such as specifications, regulations, costs, budgeting, and accounting. After a lot of work, and many failures and rewrites, he ended up with a specialised integrated software program for architects that combined business management with his CAD XT3 design program.

The three major partners in the business couldn't wait to implement the new software program and were excited when they discovered, by using this system, they could save roughly five days a month on paperwork—and it was early days; it would only get better. They suggested Paul register the software program before anyone else got hold of it, which he did.

Tom came over to Australia the following Christmas for a holiday and Paul invited him to attend the office Christmas party as his guest. Tom was rather taken with Glenda, the major partner's secretary who had organised the party. She wasn't exactly pretty but she had an interesting face and wore her long blonde hair loosely, a bit unkempt, which appealed to Tom, as did her lack of much makeup. She was also quietly spoken, with a slight lisp, which he found endearing.

'What's taking you so long to ask her out?' he whispered to Paul as Glenda moved on after offering them some canapes.

In his usual manner, Paul shrugged Tom off. 'You know what I'm like. I'll get around to it sooner or later.' However, by the end of the night, Tom had set the two of them up to go on a date.

Over a few beers at the party, Paul spoke of the success the firm had had with the computer program and how pleased they were with it. He also told Tom he'd registered it after the boss suggested he do so.

Tom grinned broadly and slapped Paul on the back. 'Well done. You won't regret it. Who knows, you might be famous one day, then Glenda will be asking *you* out.'

A few months later, Glenda came into Paul's office with her appointment book open in one hand, as she brushed her hair out of her eyes with her other hand and tucked the strands behind her ear. Her hair often fell across her face, a habit Paul found appealing. He glanced up at her and smiled.

'Paul, I've made an appointment for a guy by the name of Luke Gardener to see you next Wednesday. Sounded American. He requested the appointment specifically with you.'

'Thanks, Glenda. Wonder what he wants?'

The name didn't mean anything to Paul. He presumed he was a builder or would-be client, and he didn't give it another thought until the following Wednesday when Glenda let him know Luke Gardener was here for his ten-thirty appointment.

Paul sauntered out to the foyer and Luke extended his hand and introduced himself. He was an enormous man, easily six foot four, and wore a superbly tailored navy-blue suit with a green handkerchief in the breast pocket, a blindingly white shirt, and a green tie knotted in the American fashion. His gold cuff links caught the light as he handed his card to Paul.

Luke Gardener
Vice President
Laroke Enterprises
Palo Alto, California, USA

Luke asked if there was anywhere they could talk privately.

Paul led him into the boardroom where they sat down and indulged in a few minutes of small talk while Glenda brought in coffee. Luke finished his coffee and placed the cup gently in its saucer. He relaxed back into the big leather chair and crossed his long legs.

That is one powerful and confident-looking businessman—quite intimidating, thought Paul.

'I'll get straight to the point, Paul.' Luke said, in an American accent not unlike Tom's. 'My company is very interested in your software program, the one that incorporates business trading reports with your CAD XT3 design program.' And then, without prevarication, he said, 'We'd like to buy it from you. We'd like to employ you to help us market it and to train our customers on how it can change the way they do business.'

Inwardly, Paul was surprised; this was the very last thing he would have thought of when Glenda initially told him about the appointment. He cocked his head to one side and stared out the window, pondering what Luke had just said, wondering what to say.

At last, he spoke. 'I'd like to think about it and get back to you.' With a quizzical look on his face, he added. 'How do you even know about it?'

Luke laughed. 'My son plays bass guitar in a band with a friend of yours, Tom Watson. Tom was telling me about your program when the guys were rehearsing in our music studio recently. He had a copy of the program there and showed it to me. He thinks you're some sort of genius.' He uncrossed his long legs and leaned his elbows on the board table, casually clasping his hands together, displaying the black onyx ring on his right hand. 'Look,' he went on, 'I'm only here for a few more days. What say we meet up again tomorrow and discuss it further? Think about it—I'll answer any questions you've got then.'

'Okay. Ten-thirty tomorrow morning, here,' said Paul, and the two men stood and shook hands.

The following day, as they sat in the boardroom, Paul was the first to speak.

'I've considered your proposal and I appreciate your interest, but I don't want to become an employee of your company and work full-time in America. If I did decide to sell, I would only consider working with you as an independent contractor.'

'We may be able to work with that, but I'd like to discuss it with my colleagues. How about if we meet again tomorrow morning and see what the day brings?'

Paul left the office early. He needed to get out and run to clear his head. It was a cold afternoon, but he soon warmed up as he set a good pace and settled in for the long haul. As his head filtered out much of the superfluous stuff, he began to set priorities in his mind, the first one being to phone Tom when he got back home and ask him about Laroke and the enigmatic Mr. Gardener.

When his phone rang at one-thirty a.m. Tom woke with a fright and grabbed the phone.

'Hello, what's the problem?' Nobody rings at one-thirty a.m. unless there's a problem.

'Sorry, mate, it's me, Paul. It's seven thirty at night here and it can't wait until later. There's no problem, but I need to speak to you about something. Can you wake up and make sense please? It's important.'

Tom was instantly alert. Paul would only phone from Australia at this time if it really was important.

'What's up?'

'I've had Luke Gardener in my office yesterday and today. He wants to buy my program, and he wants my answer tomorrow. What do you know about him and this Laroke mob?'

'Well, not much, really—except they're big here in the States. They distribute video games, I think. I think Luke owns the business. They're seriously rich. His son is a buddy of mine, plays bass guitar. We've played a few gigs together. Anyway, I was over at his place recently and was chatting with his dad. We got to talking about software programs, and I told him about the one you designed and wrote. Told him you were a genius.'

Then, suddenly, as the realisation dawned, he said, 'Are you serious?' He sat bolt upright in bed, wide awake now. 'Does he really want to buy your program? That's a big deal, Paul.' Tom laughed and stifled a yawn. 'You're gonna owe me big-time if you make some money out of this. But you really need to get as much information on them as you can. Why don't you ring Dad? He's currently in Melbourne. He knows more about them than I do and I'm sure you'd benefit from his advice.'

'Good idea. I'll phone him now. Thanks, Tom. I'll let you know what happens.' Paul hung up and immediately rang Mr. Watson.

Mr. Watson listened to what Paul had to say with interest. Oh yes, he knew all about Laroke and Luke Gardener.

'Laroke is big in video games. They have systematically bought the market, buying up large companies who employ several programmers, as well as small one-man coders. They then market their games—very well, I must say—and end up with the market leaders in games. Luke Gardener is a self-made millionaire who started in advertising and saw the potential in video games when they first started. He seems to be well respected in the industry. I've met him a couple of times. Quite impressive, isn't he?'

'He certainly is,' replied Paul. 'Which is why I stalled for time before I give him an answer. If they're into video games, why would they be interested in an architectural program?'

'I've heard he's looking to diversify his business interests, which is probably why he's approached you. What's your gut feel about the situation?

Paul had been thinking long and hard about what to do. It had never occurred to him he would be approached by someone wanting to buy his program. He replied as honestly as he could, 'I'm flattered anyone would want to buy something I've designed, but at the same time, I feel reluctant to hand it over to someone else. I feel a bit vulnerable and yet I don't really understand why.'

Mr. Watson smiled to himself at the other end of the phone. Tom had been correct when he'd told him Paul was smart.

'I'll tell you one thing—Laroke is known for not negotiating. They make one offer, which is usually very generous, and that's it. It sounds like there might be a bit of travel involved as well. Why don't you wait and see what his offer is before you decide one way or the other?'

'Thanks, Mr. Watson. I feel better for having spoken with you. I'll keep you informed.'

Next day, as Paul and Luke sat in the boardroom making small talk as Glenda poured coffee, there was a certain tension in the air. Paul was aware of sitting up very straight, very focused, trying not to be intimidated by the larger-than-life Luke Gardener.

Little did he know how badly Luke Gardener wanted his program. Luke had investigated it through various channels and was excited by the thought of what Laroke could do with it. Although there were other architectural programs on the market, even ones incorporating some aspects of business management, there was nothing as comprehensive as Paul's—or as inexpensive. He loved the adrenalin rush of getting hold of something that showed such promise. He was disappointed Paul didn't want to work full-time in the States, but he was sure Paul would be okay with first-class travel and five-star hotels when he found out how much travel would be involved. If he would sell. Overnight, Luke had upped the offer he would have made yesterday. He did not want to lose this one.

'Well, Paul, my colleagues and I agree to use your services as an independent contractor. We want you to feel comfortable about working with us. I've set out our terms in this contract of sale. I'd like you to have a look at it now and let me know if we can do business together.'

Luke smiled broadly as he handed a folder to Paul. 'This is our first and final offer.'

Paul opened the folder and began to read. It was one sheet of paper, set out simply, in the centre of the page.

- Laroke Enterprises to buy outright, the Architectural and Business Management System computer program designed and written by Paul McElhone.

- Mr. McElhone will conduct training and troubleshooting for Laroke Enterprises as an independent contractor.

- Laroke Enterprises will arrange and pay for all travel—all such travel to be first-class air travel, and all hotel accommodation to be five-star accommodation.

- All Laroke Enterprises-related expenses will be paid for by Laroke Enterprises.

- Mr. McElhone will work no more than 150 days in any given year.

- Mr. McElhone will improve and update the program on a continuing basis.

- Laroke Enterprises and Mr. McElhone will honour the confidentiality of this agreement by not divulging the amount paid for the program designed and written by Mr. McElhone.

- Purchase price: $US80million.

Paul was speechless. Gobsmacked. Struck dumb. He read through it again. They had thought of everything. And the price!!! How could it possibly be worth so much? But then, Laroke would probably spend a huge amount of money marketing it worldwide at a sensible retail price, and if they could get into the market early, they could probably make a great deal of money from it.

Luke had been watching Paul closely as he read the document and knew when he reached the bottom line. But his facial expression didn't change one iota. He expected him to look up, or to look elated, or smile, but he didn't do any of those things. He'd tried to cover everything Paul could possibly have asked for, and he thought the purchase price would clinch the deal. But to get no reaction at all was worrying. Then he saw Paul read through it a second time, and then a third time. He couldn't read this young guy at all. *I wonder what excites him,* thought Luke. *Most young people would be jumping in the air by now.*

Paul looked over at Luke at last. He'd read the contract three times, stalling for time before he spoke, trying to get his heart rate down a bit, his breathing less jerky. It took him almost a minute before he felt he could speak cogently.

'You seem to have covered everything,' said Paul mildly, with no change in expression. He stood and extended his hand to Luke. 'I accept your offer, but I would like to have my lawyer take a look at the contract.'

The relief on Luke's face was discernible as they shook hands, and Paul smiled for the first time. As Luke leaned in and hugged Paul, he could feel the nervous tension in his young body. He stepped back and put both hands on Paul's shoulders.

'You will not regret this, Paul,' he said. 'We are going to work very well together, and we're both going to make a lot of money.'

And the deal was done.

Paul rang Mr. Watson as soon as he got home that night. 'I wanted to let you know I decided to sell. It's a good deal, and I don't have to live in America to comply with their conditions.'

Paul would like to have told Mr. Watson the price, but he couldn't under the terms of the confidentiality agreement.

Also, he wanted to hold on to the warm and fuzzy feeling that overwhelmed him when he got to the bottom line of the document, and he thought that feeling would disappear if everyone knew how much he'd been paid.

'Congratulations, Paul. It sounds like you're happy with your decision. And the best part is, you're still young enough and smart enough to design more programs in the future. Who knows what you might come up with further down the track? Well done.'

'Thanks for your advice last night, Mr. Watson. Always good to get an older and wiser person's opinion. I'm going to ring Tom now and tell him.'

Five minutes later, as Tom answered his call, 'I don't care what time it is in California—what colour Porsche do you want?' Paul laughed.

'You did it? You sold your program? That is fantastic, Paul. I'm really pleased for you. What did you get for it?'

'Sorry, Tom, I can't tell you under the confidentiality clause. But I feel like I've done the right thing. And I'm serious about the Porsche—this all started thanks to you. I reckon we need to celebrate. Think I'll come over for a mini holiday as soon as the sale is finalised 'cause I'm going to be working my butt off for quite a while. However, right now, I need to go for a run. Talk again soon. Bye.'

11

PAUL'S STORY—Part Two

A healthy baby boy, Michael Thomas McElhone, was born to Glenda and Paul McElhone on their third wedding anniversary. It had been a straightforward birth, and Glenda was fit and well enough to take the baby home late the following week. Her lifelong wish to be a mother fulfilled, her joy knew no bounds. She fussed over the baby and showered him with love and adoration, not to mention every type of baby paraphernalia on the market. Nothing was too good or too expensive for her son.

Michael was a good baby and easy to look after. Paul changed him and bathed him whenever Glenda asked him to, but he wasn't a natural father. He hadn't really bonded with the baby the way he hoped he would. He'd looked forward to becoming a father before Michael was born, but now the baby was home and the reality of being a parent had set in, the joy of parenthood somehow eluded Paul. He didn't feel the same way about Michael as Glenda did—her love for the baby seemed overwhelming to Paul. To her, everything in their lives revolved around the baby. Paul had never felt he was particularly significant in the world, but now he began to feel almost invisible.

When Michael was about six months old, Paul had his solicitor set up a trust fund for the child. He set it up so the fund would be locked until Michael turned eighteen, at which point the money would be released and he could spend it as he wished.

Four years later, Michael had grown into a very cheeky and unruly little boy. In Glenda's eyes, Michael could do no wrong. Whenever Paul returned home after being away, he was invariably disappointed by his son's rudeness and sense of entitlement. In Paul's eyes, Glenda spoiled Michael far more than was healthy. He was denied nothing and rarely disciplined. He took no notice of Paul when he was home—by then, the damage caused by lack of discipline, and the plethora of material things, had been done.

Scotch College in Hawthorn was known for its strict discipline and the high standard of its teaching staff, and Paul had booked Michael into the school the day they brought him home from the hospital. Paul breathed a sigh of relief when Michael started school there when he was five. The boy settled in well over the period of the first year, and there was a noticeable change in his attitude and personality.

However, Glenda missed him terribly and suggested to Paul another baby would help her get over being on her own so much, give her something to do. When she hadn't fallen pregnant within a year, the doctor referred her to a gynaecologist. Unfortunately, he found a large growth on her uterus and recommended a hysterectomy before it could develop into uterine cancer. Glenda was devastated, but she took the gynaecologist's advice and had a hysterectomy the following month. It took her several weeks to recover physically, but many months to come to terms with the fact there would be no more babies.

Life settled down to a regular pattern for the family. Although Glenda had never asked how much Paul got for his program, she knew money would never be a problem for them. She had never complained about his going away as it gave her a chance to spend the occasional weekend away with her girlfriends and enjoy various shopping trips, sometimes interstate.

They had purchased a magnificent Toorak mansion not long after they were married and Glenda had enjoyed decorating it, something she was particularly good at. When Michael started school, she completely redecorated it at a cost of nearly half a million dollars, but four years later, did the entire house over again. Glenda loved spending money.

Theirs was a comfortable, if unexciting, marriage. Their sex life was what Glenda jokingly referred to as 'vanilla,' and while Paul would have liked it to be a bit more interesting, he gave up trying to talk Glenda into trying different things early in the marriage. She was either too timid to try anything new, or she simply wasn't interested. Glenda seemed to get her kicks out of shopping—for household items, décor accessories, furniture, clothes, shoes, handbags. With serious money at her disposal, she made sure she enjoyed it.

Over the years Paul had been contracted to Laroke, he travelled extensively to the many clients who had purchased the Architectural Design and Business Admin. program. Sixty percent of the travel was within the United States, but the other forty percent took him to the UK, Scandinavia, Italy, Spain, South Africa, and Asia. He usually flew into California on his way to clients in the US and called in at the Laroke offices, sometimes taking an few extra days to catch up with Tom.

He enjoyed the travel; it was comfortable in first class, and he liked the alone time it gave him on planes and in hotels. He had stayed in some beautiful hotels around the world. The travel also afforded him the chance to run in many different and interesting places, which was the icing on the cake as far as he was concerned.

Laroke's business went from strength to strength. Video games had become more and more intricate and expensive, but that didn't impede sales in any way whatsoever. Young men couldn't get enough of them and were prepared to pay whatever the cost. Sales of CAD XT3 BMS continued to increase as the marketing and advertising of the program took off, and Luke was able to discreetly up the price, thereby making him even more profit.

At home, Paul had been playing around with some computer graphics for several months and had developed a new type of program to be used as an add-on to the original. He organised a meeting with Luke on his next trip to the States.

As Paul stepped out of the elevator on the fifteenth floor of the Laroke Enterprises building into the plush, beautifully decorated management suite, Luke walked out of his glass-walled corner office and greeted him.

'Well, look who's here! Good to see you, Paul. I believe we've got a meeting. Is that a laptop I see you've got under your arm?'

'Good to see you too, Luke. And it is indeed a laptop. Wait until you see what's on it.' Paul gave a sly little smile as he spoke, like someone with a surprise birthday present who knows it's going to be well received.

The two men shook hands, and Luke led Paul into the boardroom. He poured coffee for both of them from the ever-ready percolator and carried them over to the table. They sat comfortably at the huge boardroom table, Luke at the head of the table, Paul at right angles to him. Luke was very interested to know what Paul wanted to talk about. He presumed it must be important for Paul to arrange a meeting, especially since he usually just breezed in, had a chat, and breezed out. He felt mildly concerned but didn't want to show it. He began to tap his foot, an action his staff knew to be a sign of impatience.

Luke sat back from the table and crossed his long legs as an alternative to the foot-tapping, then took a mouthful of the hot coffee. 'So, what's up, Paul?' Luke didn't believe in the soft approach. He liked to get straight to the point.

Paul casually took a sip of his coffee and opened his laptop. He turned it slightly so Luke could see the screen easily. 'I've got something I'd like to show you, something I've been working on for a while,' he said mildly as he tapped on a couple of keys. A program opened; he tapped on a few more keys and a picture of an architecturally modern house filled the screen.

'Mmm,' mused Luke. 'Show me something I haven't seen before.' He kept the annoyance out of his voice. He had a busy day ahead, and he hoped this wasn't going to waste too much of his time.

'Okay,' said Paul, tapping a few more keys. Suddenly, the picture on the screen turned 180 degrees and the bare, unfurnished interior of the living room appeared.

Luke could feel himself getting interested. Perhaps this wasn't going to be a waste of time after all. He sat up straight, leaned forward, resting his elbows on the table. 'That's clever. Can you do it for other parts of a building?'

'Sure,' said Paul. He clicked on another part of the house and the bathroom appeared, bare of all fittings and furnishings. Another click, and there was the empty kitchen.

'Did you invent this, Paul?' Luke asked, trying to keep his excitement in check

'Sure did,' said Paul. 'But wait, there's more.' Back to the living room. 'How about we furnish it?' Another click, and dark timber floorboards appeared. Another click, and beautiful oriental rugs graced the floor. Another click, and a leather lounge and armchairs. Another click, and lamps appeared, and with another click, and the lamps lit up. Next a TV; then a coffee table.

'Don't like timber floor and rugs?' Paul went on. 'Let's change them.' Click, click, carpet! 'Don't like the colour of the lounge? We can change it.' Click, click, a different colour! 'How about some drapes?' Click, click, drapes, pelmet, tiebacks! Not only was the program effective, but the furnishings were incredibly realistic, complete with shadows and weather conditions. It made the property look like something out of *Architectural Digest*.

Luke stood, his excited demeanour like a kid at a birthday party. He couldn't take his eyes off the screen. 'This is amazing, Paul. We can do great things with this. What's your price?'

At this stage, Paul could have said any figure and Luke wouldn't have hesitated. But instead, Paul said, 'I've got all the money I need. But I'd like to feel part of the success of Laroke. I've watched your business grow into a very successful corporation. I believe it's going to be around for a very long time, and I'd like to share in its success. I'd like a minor interest in the business in return for this program.'

Luke was surprised. It was the last thing he would have imagined, but when he thought about it, that was Paul to a T. He wasn't in it for the money; he was too smart for that. He was prepared to back his creation, which was why Luke was delighted to have him on board.

'How about we start with ten percent and grow together?' said Luke as he extended his hand. A wide grin spread across Paul's face as they shook hands and consolidated the deal.

After graduating high school with excellent grades, Michael entered university to study chemistry. His mother and father had been very proud of his final marks, and while Glenda congratulated him and showered him with kisses and told him how much she loved him, Paul still found it difficult to express himself where Michael was concerned. He shook his hand and said, 'Congratulations, Michael, well done.' And bought him a new car.

Midway through his second year at uni, Michael came home early one day when he knew his mum and dad would both be home. They were sitting under the graceful white pergola on the sandstone terrace at the back of the house in the big comfortable cane chairs, enjoying afternoon tea in the beautifully manicured back garden.

Michael grabbed a Coke out of the fridge and walked out onto the terrace.

'Hi, Mum,' he said, bending down to kiss Glenda's cheek. 'Hi, Dad.' He took a swig of Coke and glanced around the garden. 'I've got some news for you. You know how much I've wanted to get out on my own, well, yesterday, I signed a lease on an apartment in Docklands. I'll move out in about three weeks.' He paused for a moment. 'I hope you don't mind too much, Mum,' he added, to soften the blow, which he knew Glenda would feel acutely.

'Oh, Michael, of course I mind. Eighteen is so young. Why on earth would you want to move out of home? You've got everything you want here; your meals are cooked for you, your washing and ironing is done. Have you thought about those things? Have you thought this through? Why don't you stay here another year and then think about it?'

But she could see he had thought about it. Why else would he have already signed a lease? 'We'll miss you terribly,' she said, accepting the decision was made. She could feel her lip tremble. *Don't cry, don't cry*, she thought. *He won't like that.*

'I'm eighteen now, Mum. I can access my trust fund so I can afford to move out. And yes, I've thought about all those things you mentioned. I've got to learn to cook sooner or later, so it might as well be now. You'll love the apartment, and I want you to come over as soon as I've got my stuff sorted.'

He smiled and hugged his mother, but he could see she was distraught at the thought of his moving out. He knew she'd be like this, but he was determined to follow through and not let them talk him out of it, which was why he waited until he'd signed the lease before he told them.

Paul shook his hand and wished him well. 'I'm sure you'll make a go of it, Son,' he said. 'I'm happy to help you move if you want me to. Eighteen is a bit young to move out of home, but you won't be eighteen for long. Good luck.'

The house seemed strangely quiet once Michael had packed up and moved out, not that he was ever very noisy. Perhaps empty more than quiet. Glenda missed him more than Paul could have imagined and could not be consoled. Fortunately, Paul was home at the moment, but he was concerned. He had a planned trip to South Africa the following month. How would she handle being on her own then?

But this was their life now. This was the 'next stage.'

At first, Michael came home every week for dinner, and Glenda was a different person when he was there. She constantly told him she loved him and asked him to come home more often, but he was busy making a life of his own as kids do when they move out. Then every week became every second week and eventually, every third or fourth week.

Six months later, Glenda still hadn't come to grips with Michael not being upstairs studying or lounging around in the family room, watching TV and drinking a beer or bringing some mates home for a game of snooker in the billiard room. Paul didn't understand how or why she was always so down; he didn't get it. For him, it seemed so peaceful in the house with just the two of them, and although he wouldn't admit it out loud, he didn't miss Michael. Even though he was his son, Paul had never found it easy to talk to Michael—they had never really had a meaningful conversation. Perhaps, deep down, they were more alike than Paul realised.

As time went by, Glenda found consolation in buying stuff, not just clothes and homewares in retail shops, but she would sit for hours watching the Shopping Channel and buy more things over the internet: a Kitchen Whiz (she already had two in the butler's pantry); an electric gadget that, when used on the face, was as good as a face-lift; a second, and very unnecessary, outdoor setting for the back deck; and an oriental rug for $15,500. Although Paul was slightly concerned when parcels kept arriving and Glenda returned from a shopping trip with lots of various store bags in tow, he thought, *if that's what she wants to do, and money isn't a problem, then let her have her fun. She obviously gets enjoyment from all this stuff.*

But it was only a matter of time before a scene unfolded that was beyond Paul's comprehension.

His phone rang.

'Paul, it's me.' Glenda's voice was hard to recognise through the crying. 'Paul, I'm in trouble. Can you please come down to Prahran Police Station straightaway?'

'Are you hurt?'

'No, I need you to come down here now.'

'Okay, I'm on my way.'

When he arrived at the police station, Paul was ushered into an interview room where Glenda sat across the desk from a policeman who was making notes.

'What seems to be the problem?' Paul asked the policeman, as he stood behind Glenda and softly rested his hand on her shoulder to reassure her. She immediately jumped up and threw herself into his arms, wrapping her arms around his neck.

'Oh, Paul. I'm sorry. I'm so sorry,' she sobbed, hanging on to him.

'It's okay,' Paul said as he tried to pry her arms from around his neck. 'Let me find out what's going on.'

'So, what's this all about?' he asked, a second time.

'Your wife has been caught shoplifting, Mr. McElhone. We received a call from the David Jones store in Malvern a short while ago. We've read Mrs. McElhone her rights, and she wanted to phone you.'

Paul was struck dumb, momentarily blind-sided. Shoplifting! Why would Glenda want to pinch anything? She had an unlimited credit card and always had plenty of cash on her. 'Is this true? What did you take?' he asked Glenda in utter bewilderment.

'A lipstick, and some mascara, and some foundation, and other stuff.' Glenda had let go of Paul and had sat back down opposite the policeman. She suddenly looked very sheepish and contrite, like a small child, eyes downcast, twisting a tissue in her hands. The sobbing had eased, and she had regained some of her composure.

Paul was shocked. He had expected her to deny she had ever taken anything. It was obviously a mistake, and would he please fix it?

The policeman caught the attention of a policewoman who was walking past the open door. 'Oh, Constable Stewart, would you mind taking Mrs. McElhone into the mess room and making her a cup of tea? I'm sure she could use a cup of tea right now.' Constable Stewart smiled gently at Glenda and took her arm, leading her out of the room and down the hallway.

'Sit down, Mr. McElhone,' said the policeman kindly. 'I'm Senior Constable Rick Stratton, by the way. I realise it's patently obvious Mrs. McElhone didn't take the goods because she couldn't afford to pay for them. We see this type of incident from time to time, and it's usually a sign of something not quite right elsewhere in the offender's life. I think your wife might benefit from talking to a professional who is used to dealing with this type of thing.

He handed a card to Paul. 'I can recommend this psychiatrist. He handles cases such as your wife's constantly, and to my knowledge, has helped several people with similar problems. If you'll agree to her undergoing counselling, we won't take this case any further. No charges will be laid. Are you in agreement with this suggestion?'

'Of course,' replied Paul. 'I'll arrange for her to see him immediately. She hasn't been her usual self since our son moved out of home a few months ago. I think it may help her to talk to someone about it. Thanks for your help. I appreciate it.'

As they drove home, Paul put his hand on Glenda's knee and said, 'Don't beat yourself up about this. Apparently, it's not uncommon. It's not the end of the world. We'll make an appointment for you to see Dr. Golinski as soon as possible and I'm sure he'll be able to help you.'

Glenda squeezed Paul's hand and smiled shyly. 'I feel better already. Thank you for being so understanding, Paul.'

A routine developed where Glenda saw Dr. Golinski every three weeks, and soon life reverted to normal once more. The shoplifting incident had given Paul a shock. It had caused a ripple on the smooth waters of his life, but those waters had settled back down into a glassy stillness—still on the surface, but deep. And dark.

After twenty-five years of working and travelling, Paul occasionally reflected on his life, particularly when he was sitting up at the front of the plane enjoying a glass of champagne. It had been an easy life financially since he sold his program to Laroke twenty-five years ago, and the travel always buoyed him.

But when he returned home, he would sometimes feel a type of dullness, a feeling that, at age fifty-three, even though he had everything money could buy and had travelled the world, life was passing him by. His marriage to Glenda was comfortable, if unexciting, and he was not unhappy, but he had a nagging thought in the back of his mind that his life lacked something, something intangible. It was as if he'd achieved everything the material world had to offer and there was nothing left to strive for. The future was more of the same, day in, day out. He had never been a people person, and as much as he loved working on his computer programs, he hadn't felt excited by anything in an awfully long time.

Is this the feeling that comes with age? Is this what being fifty-three is all about? Is this all there is? These kinds of thoughts didn't linger, didn't bother him unduly, but they returned often, sometimes while he was sitting in his favourite armchair reading the Saturday papers.

Which is what he was doing when he came across the newspaper article on web addresses and how they were sometimes misleading. He smiled to himself. He remembered reading an article a while ago about a website set up by a group of psychologists with the unfortunate address: www.therapistsacademy.com. As he was reading the article, he picked up his iPad and entered one of the addresses in the newspaper article—www.letsbefriends.com. The page opened and he could see immediately it was a site where men and women could meet up for more than friendship. This particular 'let's be friends' actually meant 'let's be friends with benefits.' He casually read through some of the profiles of ladies wanting to meet men, and his interest was piqued. *Dangerous, but interesting.* He read on. *Dangerous, but very interesting. Some of these women are outrageous! Oh, here's one who lives here in Melbourne. No picture, virtually no information, except she's fifty and is interested in politics, sport, reading, and people.*

Before he had time to think it through, he'd signed in and written a brief profile of himself. He clicked on the woman who had supplied no information about herself but was interested in politics, sport, and reading. It didn't get much more anonymous!

In all his married life, Paul had never strayed. Never been game enough. He was timid by nature, not what you'd call adventurous. But on the internet, it was different. You weren't face-to-face with a female, struggling for something to say, embarrassed in case they thought you were an idiot. You had more time to think before replying to an email. He didn't want a relationship; he was happy with the one he had. But the thought of connecting with someone, especially someone of the opposite sex, whom you were never going to meet, was somehow stimulating, thought provoking.

And right now, his life needed some stimulation, some excitement.

He typed an email to her and hit Send.

What could possibly go wrong?

12

THE AFFAIR

The first email Karen received from Paul was brief but seemed honest, self-deprecating.

I'm 53 years old, married with one son, physically fit, active and healthy.

I live in the inner east and work primarily in Richmond writing specialist software.

I'm probably going through what's laughingly referred to as a male mid-life crisis, except it's not really funny.

If you reply to this, I'll give thanks to the Gods of Letter Writing.

Karen put it to one side, meaning to reply to it later, but forgot about it.

A few weeks later, she received a second email from Paul reminding her she had not yet replied to him. *This guy might come across as self-deprecating, but he also has guts—I wouldn't have followed up on anyone who didn't reply to me!*

She eventually replied, without apology, and asked him to tell her a little more about himself. A week later, she received his reply.

Word picture of me:
calm
conservative
taciturn
patient
persistent—you might have picked up on that already
with a sense of humour
non-violent
naïve
indecisive…I think
And now it's your turn

Well, she did ask for it! She replied the following week with a word portrait of herself.

Sense of humour
Likes people
Stubborn
Careful
Thoughtful
Kind
A bit mad

And so, they began emailing each other once or twice a week.

Emails from Paul were usually very brief. He told her his name was Paul McElhone and in one email, included his mobile phone number. A week or two went by and Karen began to wonder what his voice sounded like. Curiosity eventually got the better of her and she dialled his mobile number.

When he answered, he knew instantly it was Karen and he said in a bit of a rush, 'It's exciting to hear your voice, to speak to you. I feel like I've won a prize.' There was a pause as Paul considered what to say next. 'I've never done anything like this before. I never had much success with the opposite sex, even when I was young, so I'm not sure what happens next.'

Karen took this with a grain of salt and presumed it was a line he used whenever the occasion arose, but when she thought about it, here she was, doing the same thing— and she'd never done anything like this before, either.

'Me neither,' she said with a laugh, and hung up.

But he had sounded so sweet, so naïve. She emailed him within the next five minutes.

Do you understand the risks involved in an internet relationship? I presume your wife doesn't know you're writing to a woman. What would happen if she found out?

His reply was:

I wasn't planning on getting caught!

Naïve in the extreme!

They exchanged photos. It was a good photo of him, a straight-on head shot. Not bad looking, with a pleasant smile and an open face. He had a bit of a twinkle in the eye, curly hair going grey and thinning a bit. She dug out the best recent one of her and emailed it to him. 'Nice' was his underwhelming reply.

They continued the back-and-forth emails, becoming more relaxed with each other and sometimes cheeky. He had a funny sense of humour, was quick-witted and clever, which she liked. When she asked him about his hobbies, he replied he only had one significant hobby and that was running. When pushed, he elaborated: the first marathon-type race he had entered had been the half-marathon at the Melbourne Festival. The following year he had run the full marathon, and had subsequently run the New York City Marathon, the London Marathon, the Boston Marathon, and the Berlin Marathon. This was a person who took running very seriously.

A couple of months later, she received the following email from Paul:

Would you like to meet for lunch?

Not the most elegant lunch invitation she'd ever received, but at least it was straightforward. Faced with a decision she knew she would have to make eventually, she decided to declare herself.

Paul, I'm sorry, but I lied on my profile about a few things. My real name is Karen Cosgrove, and I don't live in Victoria, I live in NSW. I'm not fifty, I'm fifty-eight. Please take time to think about this revelation. I realise this makes me seem paranoid, but I was being careful. I am always hesitant about sending anything over the internet.

I completely understand if you want to cease all contact, just be straight forward about it and say so, no excuse necessary.

His cheeky reply made her laugh:

I can understand why anyone who lived in NSW would lie about it—Victoria is a much better place to live.

Age doesn't mean much to me, but on the other hand, perhaps I could learn something from an 'older' woman.

And yes, I would definitely like to continue writing to you.

During the next few months, their emails became more regular and Paul and Karen shared many internet chats about life, politics, climate change, and the world at large. He showed an interest when Karen told him she painted. He seemed knowledgeable on painters and paintings, both modern and the masters. He didn't volunteer any personal information, but when Karen asked, Paul told her his wife's name was Glenda, and that his son, Michael, had moved out of home years ago, so it was just the two of them. When she pressed further, he said his marriage was fine, but he felt life was passing him by and he wanted a bit of excitement in his life before he woke up one morning and realised it was too late.

As they became more comfortable and less guarded with each other, their internet relationship became enjoyable. Karen couldn't wait for Paul's next email to pop up in her inbox. She thought of him often, wondering what his home life was like, what his wife was like, why he didn't get on with his son, wanting to know more about this new 'man in her life.' She didn't like to ask too many questions as Paul rarely, if ever, asked her questions about her life. What he knew about her was what she had chosen to tell him.

Occasionally, Paul would make a cheeky comment and Karen would retaliate, until their emails eventually became more intimate, sharing private personal information and innuendo. She opened her inbox one morning and there was an email from Paul and her heart did a little dance. She clicked on the email.

Thought the attachment was relevant. xx

She opened the attachment. It was an MP3 file. She clicked on it and Paul's voice sang 'When I Woke Up This Morning, You Were on My Mind.' Karen laughed and laughed, and then she smiled smugly to herself. *Mmmm, nice.*

Paul also eagerly awaited Karen's next email. He began to fantasize about her, wondered what she would be like in bed and how he could get her there. It was a feeling he hadn't experienced before, even when younger. Life had always been about other things—the business, family, money and how to handle it. This was new to him, and it made his day-to-day life more interesting, more stimulating, more fun. The only other time he'd ever felt this excitement was when he discovered Taliesin West and architecture.

Simmering away below the surface was the desire to meet her.

A few months after they began corresponding, Karen was due to visit her cousin and his wife in Melbourne. Martin didn't get on with her cousin so she went down on her own a couple of times a year. She looked forward to these trips—it was a week away from Martin, plus she and her cousin had been close as kids and she enjoyed catching up with him and his wife every so often.

She mentioned the upcoming trip in an email to Paul.

Guess what? I'm coming down to Melbourne in a few weeks to see my cousin and his wife. Imagine, crossing the border to the funny little state of Victoria!

He replied the next day.

Can I take you to lunch whilst you're here? You never know what might happen if we actually met!

A second email from him followed immediately.

Please don't worry—I'm very easy to say no to.

A ripple of excitement ran through Karen as she read the email. Clearly, he was as apprehensive about meeting her as she was about meeting him, and what may follow. By now she desperately wanted to meet him, but was this a step too far? In her entire married life, she had never contemplated infidelity, but now it was all she could think about.

When John had left her all those years ago, she had been in love with him and thought she would never know that feeling again. Then, when she met and married Martin, she felt safe in the knowledge she could have a good life, even though she didn't love him. She didn't think for one moment that very situation would make her vulnerable if she ever met another man to whom she was attracted.

She agreed to meet Paul in Melbourne.

They met at a prearranged place in the city and recognised each other instantly.

'Hello at last', said Karen. 'Hi', said Paul, at exactly the same time.

They both laughed with embarrassment and shook hands. Karen noticed both of their hands were sweaty and a bit shaky. The sexual tension between them was palpable; electricity sparked between the two.

'Can I buy you a coffee?'

'Great idea. I need one to steady my nerves', Karen laughed, as they walked towards the Botanic Gardens. *He must now think I'm an idiot,* thought Karen. *Fancy suggesting coffee would steady anyone's nerves!*

Karen was struck by Paul's appearance. He wasn't a tall man—five foot nine at most—and slightly built. He wore a gold signet ring on the little finger of his right hand and what looked like a rather expensive gold watch. His clothes were well tailored; he was wearing navy slacks and an open-necked, beautifully cut, cream linen shirt over which he wore a linen jacket and brown loafers. His look was casual and understated, and it suited him.

It was a beautiful summer's day and once inside the gardens they soon found a place to have coffee. They sat under a huge Liquid Amber tree in dappled sunlight and, as she relaxed, Karen chatted easily while Paul mostly listened. But constantly in the background was the spectre of 'what next?'

After a pause in the conversation, both spoke simultaneously: 'Well, what do you reckon?'

They laughed nervously and Paul whispered, 'I'm game if you are.'

Karen shocked both herself and Paul by saying, 'I can't wait.'

In anticipation, and hope, of this moment, Paul had already booked a hotel room, just in case, and they took a cab to the hotel. Neither said a word in the cab but jumbled thoughts filled Karen's head: *What the hell am I doing? I'm going to a hotel with a man I met a couple of hours ago. He could be a serial rapist for all I know. I can't believe I'm doing this.*

Then, once inside the hotel, as Paul led her down the plush hotel corridor to Room 1237, she thought, *It's not too late to* pull out. On the other hand, he could be thinking the same thing. I could turn out to be a bunny boiler for all he knows.*

It was a room on a high floor of a five-star hotel overlooking the city, and the sun streamed in the window. Karen walked over to the window to have a look at the view, and also because she didn't know what else to do. She could hear her heart pumping in her ears, and she could feel sweat trickling down the centre of her back. *God, I hope it's not showing through my dress*, she thought. *That's such an ugly look.*

Then: *It's still not too late to back out. Why should I care if he thinks I'm an idiot? I'll never see him again.*

Then, as she concentrated on taking deep breaths and her breathing became more regular: *But this is so exciting. It's like a movie—what happens next?*

The room was silent, but filled with atmosphere and anticipation, and when Paul walked over and stood behind her, she slowly turned to face him. He put his arms around her and gently drew her to him in a warm hug.

As Karen's arms automatically wrapped themselves around his neck, she was overcome by the most incredible feeling. Like coming home. Like finding the centre of your being. Like a drink of cool water after days in the desert. She could have stood there in that soft embrace forever. It was magical.

Karen thought she could feel Paul trembling, but she sensed he felt the sweetness of the embrace, too. After what seemed like hours standing there, still and silent, he took her hand and led her to the bed.

They were both so nervous, so tightly wound, what followed was a disaster. It seemed so contrived, so full of the expectation of perfect lovemaking, there was no hope of it being anything but a fumbling, hot, sweaty mishmash of bodies. Karen imagined it was similar to teenage kids experiencing their first attempt at sex. It had been so long since Karen and Martin had been intimate, she was unsure of herself, lacked the confidence to handle this surreal scenario. All she could think about was Paul must have regretted the moment he'd suggested they meet.

She was quiet as they left the hotel and felt responsible for what had turned into an awkward situation. If Paul was disappointed, he was too much of a gentleman to show it. When they said goodbye that afternoon, although they smiled, and he kissed her on the cheek, she didn't ever expect to hear from him again.

When her phone rang early the next morning, she was astonished it was Paul. She hardly had a chance to say hello before he said, 'Yes, Hi.' He then rushed on, 'Karen, I had such a great time yesterday. I can't wait to see you again. Can we meet today?'

Karen was surprised and a bit nonplussed. Why would it be any better today? But deep in her belly, she wanted to see him, wanted to experience again the magical feeling that had enveloped her when they first embraced.

They agreed to meet in the Gardens at the same time as yesterday. Karen arrived about five minutes early and stood in the shade of one of the enormous fig trees. Deep in thought of the coming day, she hadn't realised she was smiling until one passer-by smiled back at her and called a cheery 'Good Morning.'

As he approached her, Paul looked very serious and Karen half-expected bad news of some sort. Instead, he spoke quickly and quietly, almost frowning. 'Do you want coffee?' he asked. 'I don't want coffee. I want to kiss you and feel your body next to mine. I can't wait to touch you, to kiss you, to lie naked with you.' He took her face in his hands and kissed her mouth, gently, tenderly. Then, 'Please tell me you don't want coffee.'

When she could at last speak, she stammered, 'I d-definitely don't want c-coffee.'

He led her to his car, opened the door for her, then proceeded to drive quite fast to the hotel. Karen was surprised when she saw the car. Although she didn't know much about cars, she recognized it as a late-model Porsche and for the second time in two days, the thought flitted through her mind: Paul was wealthy.

Once in the hotel room, Paul was determined to help Karen relax and enjoy their time together. He was so gentle and took the time to make sure she felt comfortable with what they were doing. He wasn't nervous today; by contrast, he was the consummate lover. By the time he entered her, the nerve endings all over her body were tingling with anticipation. It could not have been more perfect.

By the end of the afternoon, they agreed it had been a sublime day and one they'd like to repeat at some time in the future.

The following week, back home in Coffs, Karen and Paul continued their correspondence by email, which became more frequent and intimate. They became infatuated with each other. Their emails were flirtatious and often funny and progressed to being very sexy indeed.

Three or four months after her trip to Melbourne, Karen arranged to go to Sydney for a quick break. When she mentioned this to Paul, he told her he could get away for a couple of days and meet her there. When she agreed, he booked them into the top hotel overlooking the Harbour for two nights. It was during these two delightful days and nights their relationship morphed into the 'honeymoon' stage, and they had a truly wonderful time—sexually liberating and socially very enjoyable.

Once back home and submerged in everyday life, Karen often thought of how she had become entranced with sex with Paul. Their time together was so different from anything she had experienced before. She had never felt this way about sex with either John or Martin, had never enjoyed it particularly, certainly not the way she enjoyed it with Paul. She had never thought about it, dreamed about it, wanted it so much. Paul's body fascinated her. Although he was very slim, he was in extremely good shape, with flawless olive skin. They were a snug fit together. She loved to run her hands over his smooth skin, examine the fine hair on his powerful forearms. His once dark hair was greying at the temples and it gave him a gentle, mellow look, which was highlighted by the dark brown, slightly hooded eyes. Although not traditionally handsome, there was something very appealing about the overall look of him. He glowed with good health and always looked comfortable and relaxed.

Paul felt the same way about Karen—couldn't get enough of her. His mind constantly filled with thoughts of her, her body, her enthusiasm, and her lack of inhibitions when she was with him. She supplied everything missing in his 'real world' life. What he wanted more than anything else, and what was missing from his life, was to be wanted, desired physically, and Karen was not bashful about showing her desire for him, his body, his sex.

As much as Paul loved his wife, she had lost interest in sex, and although she didn't deny him, it had become a chore for her. It wasn't a chore for Karen. When they were together, she wanted him, totally. And he made sure she was completely satisfied and wholly enjoyed their sex life.

Time away with Paul was a complete escape from reality. He would always book a suite in the same five-star hotel overlooking Sydney Harbour and insisted on paying for everything. They usually met up at the airport and took a cab together to the hotel where the routine was always the same: prepare a bath, open a bottle of wine. The pair of them would lie in the bath, drinking wine and talking about the next two days and nights.

On one such occasion, Paul stretched out between Karen's legs, his back sliding up against her chest in the warm bath as he turned off the tap with his right foot. She soaped his back and began to massage his shoulders, kneading her thumbs into the base of his skull, feeling the muscles there begin to relax and soften.

She leaned forward until her mouth was near his ear and in a soft, sexy voice, asked 'Would you like me to wash your hair?'

'I'd love you to,' he whispered, as a small smile escaped his lips and he sighed deeply, in anticipation of what was going to happen.

Karen opened the miniature bottle of hotel shampoo and squeezed some into her hand. Its silky smoothness smelled good as she rubbed it between her hands. Starting at the crown, she slowly rubbed the pearly substance into Paul's hair, round and round, making sure the shampoo was disbursed evenly over his skull. Using all ten fingers, she started above his ears, massaging firmly and rhythmically, making little circles, lifting the hair, increasing the pressure. Down onto his forehead, his temples, up under his jawline and throat.

Paul could feel the tension ooze out of his body with every movement. Nothing relaxed him like one of Karen's head massages. *This must be what nirvana feels like*, he thought. *Peaceful, transcendental, hypnotic.*

'Mmm. Feels good,' he sighed.

She reached for the spare drinking glass she'd placed at the side of the bath, scooped up some warm bathwater, and poured it over his head, rinsing off the suds a couple of times until the water ran clear.

By the time they had climbed out of the bath and dried each off with the hotel's fluffy towels, they were well and truly in the mood for bed—the king-sized, comfortable soft bed with its cool, fresh, white bed linen. How wonderful—no time constraints, no rush, just take-your-time sex.

They went shopping together and Paul bought her several sets of beautiful, sexy underwear, which she would wear, and slowly remove, for him. He bought her a black leather corset outfit that laced up at the front—oh, how he loved undoing those laces! They were uninhibited in their lovemaking, as if they were each making up for lost time and enjoyment.

Karen figured he must have been very unhappy with his sex life at home to risk contacting anyone on the internet. She had presumed at first, because he was rich, he could get any woman he wanted, but as she got to know him, Karen realised Paul lacked confidence when it came to women and was significantly introverted.

She believed him when he said he had never been unfaithful in his marriage. She doubted he had ever made a serious pass at another woman face-to-face. When he was on his computer, he was in his world, in control. But chatting to a lady on the internet or even over the phone was one thing; suggesting they meet would have been a big step for Paul.

He was correct when he'd said he was not much of a conversationalist, which appealed to Karen, who lived with someone who chatted constantly. Even though conversations with Martin were often entertaining and he made her laugh, when Karen had to occasionally ask Martin to please stop talking, he could only maintain the silence for a short while.

But Paul was a quiet man by nature, a thinker who kept his thoughts to himself. He was a gentle soul, almost timid, and although Karen liked his unassertive persona, she knew she could never rely on him to defend her in a threatening or dangerous situation.

One thing she found particularly unusual about him was he didn't seem to mind what other people did or thought. Not much bothered him. This had its downside though—he seemed to live his life on the one level, no highs or lows, just a straight line. She never heard him complain, but she couldn't discover exactly what or who he admired in life, either. It was as if he couldn't let himself go, and always kept himself in check. At times he seemed worldly and sophisticated; other times, he seemed disappointed in life, as if his inner self was asking: *Is this all there is?*

On one occasion, when they were in Sydney together for a couple of days, Paul's phone rang as they were getting dressed to go out for lunch. It was the first time Karen had ever heard it ring. To her knowledge, he had never taken a call while they had been away together, not even from his wife. Paul answered but said very little. A shadow passed over his face as he finished the call.

'That was my wife's psychiatrist. Apparently, my wife didn't show for her appointment this morning, and she's not answering her phone. I'll try her phone.'

Alarm bells rang in Karen's head when she heard the word *psychiatrist*. She had no idea Paul's wife was seeing a psychiatrist. She walked over to the window as he dialled the number and tried not to appear to be listening.

'Hi. Any reason you didn't make your appointment this morning?' he asked casually. Pause. Then: 'Well, don't worry. I'll be home tonight and we can talk about it then.' And he hung up.

He walked over to where Karen was standing, looking out over the harbour. 'Sorry about that,' he said. 'My wife has a few mental health issues.'

'You don't have to tell me, Paul,' Karen said. 'You don't have to explain anything to me.'

He sat on the bed and leaned his elbows on his knees, running his hands through his hair. 'Probably best if you know,' he said. 'My wife was caught shoplifting a few years ago and has been seeing a psychiatrist regularly ever since. She certainly wasn't shoplifting because she couldn't afford what she wanted; it was more to get attention. She's had trouble adjusting ever since our son moved out of home. I think it's generally referred to as the 'Empty Nest Syndrome.' She often has trouble differentiating between what's real and what's not. Exaggerates, tells lies—except for her, they're not lies.'

Karen didn't know what to make of this information, but she suddenly felt very sorry for Paul. No wonder he was looking for something outside his marriage to give him a bit of a break from his 'real' world.

And suddenly, out of the doom and gloom of the tension-filled atmosphere, he jumped up and said, 'Come on. Let's go and get some lunch.'

After many hours spent thinking about him and trying to analyse Paul, Karen concluded, for her, their relationship was about much more than the sex. She really enjoyed spending time with him. He was such a calm and peaceful person. This calmness transferred itself to Karen whenever they met, and the feeling stayed with her for several days.

Whenever they had met up in Sydney and spent a couple of days and nights in a suite at the hotel Paul always booked, and it was time to go, Paul was invariably packed and ready first. He would sit quietly looking out of the window as Karen showered and dressed. If he was ever annoyed because she took her time getting ready, he certainly never showed it.

But then she was convinced he simply didn't feel annoyance, or anger, or frustration—or joy, or vibrancy, or sheer excitement either. When they were together, or emailing each other, or when they chatted on the internet, they would discuss many things—life, politics, sex, even football. They didn't always agree, but voices were never raised. There was never any anger or sarcasm in their exchanges.

In the early days, Karen presumed the reason Paul was so wealthy was because he was good at his job. He hadn't told her in any detail about his business, and she hadn't asked, but she had gleaned he was a computer whiz with design skills, a rare combination, and he must have made a lot of money utilizing these skills in the architectural field.

Eventually, they began to talk about their careers in more detail, their childhoods, and those early growing-up days in their lives. Paul explained to her how he had invented a software program many years ago that enabled architects not only to design and draw plans on a computer but to integrate their costs and profits at the same time. He pointed out there were a couple of other similar programs on the market at the time, but his program was simpler to operate and much cheaper. He had sold it to the Americans for a good price, which had set him up for life. He worked constantly on the program, modifying and improving it, and because he travelled a great deal troubleshooting and managing the program for architectural clients in various parts of the world, he was away from home a lot of the time.

'I kind of feel responsible for my wife's loneliness, which probably contributed to her problems.'

'Are you fully present when you're home?' Karen asked.

'I try to be, but you know I'm not much of a talker,' was his reply, and he deftly changed the subject to avoid going any deeper into a subject that involved feelings.

One thing she really enjoyed during the time she and Paul spent together was they both loved playing cards and doing puzzles. Paul excelled at card games. He had such a quick mind; he could count the cards as they fell. He excelled at any games or puzzles based on numbers, although Karen could sometimes beat him at quizzes, especially current affairs. Paul taught her the rudiments of chess, but it would take her quite a few years to even begin to understand the game properly.

'How come you're so good at numbers?' Karen asked him. 'You're a natural.' She was amazed at this talent; he was better than anyone she had ever known.

Paul gave a wry smile and said, 'I got my degree in Mathematics at Melbourne Uni before I discovered architecture. Then, a bit later in life, I did my PhD in Computer Science—love those zeros and ones!' He laughed and looked bashful, almost embarrassed to tell anyone about how smart he was.

'So, you're Dr. McElhone? As well as a qualified architect?' Karen asked in amazement.

'Yeah. I like studying. I enjoy the concentrated effort. Really focuses the mind.'

And that was the end of the discussion. He was probably a genius, but he was so self-deprecating he would never have told her had she not asked.

For all the feelings of love, infatuation, call it what you will, Karen had for Paul, she knew they would never make it together out in the real world. She could never live with him. He was the most self-contained man she had ever known, living completely within himself. He never asked questions of her, which, in a way, was handy—Karen had only ever told him what she wanted him to know. Karen was disappointed he didn't want to know more about her. He lived in the moment, as if the past was the past, a closed subject after the event.

He could sometimes be cold and distant, and he seemed unable to, or didn't want to, talk about feelings—his or others'. He lacked empathy.

Karen told Paul about her first love, John, and how his leaving had affected her. Those distant memories came rushing back as she talked about their relationship, and at one stage, she became misty eyed. Paul seemed completely unmoved by her heightened emotional state, and she said, 'Have you ever been hurt by someone you loved?'

And he replied, 'I've never felt that strongly about anyone.'

Ah, that straight line again. No ups, no downs, no river deep, no mountain high.

And yet they understood each other well. Karen made no demands of him, nor he of her. When they were together, there was no tension, no mind games, no hurry. Just relaxation of all senses. It was a very unusual relationship. They had never been found out. Their relationship had never been discovered. Neither one of them had ever spoken to another person about the other, and neither of them ever criticised their partner to the other.

Once, when they were lying in bed snuggled up together, to her complete surprise, Paul asked, 'Do you love me?'

Karen hesitated a moment, not sure how to answer. Neither of them had ever mentioned the 'L' word. She quickly gathered her thoughts and replied, 'Within these four walls, I love you more than any man I've ever known.'

But I don't need you, she thought to herself.

Karen had loved John and was shattered when he left her. She didn't ever expect to fall in love again, didn't want to. But being with Paul filled her with the longing and excitement she had never dreamed of all those years ago when she married Martin.

Being with Paul was the 'other path' she mulled over in her quiet moments. Not a permanent path, but the risky, breathtaking, thrilling excitement she had wanted to experience.

But realistically, she knew they would not have lasted long as a couple.

She needed more than Paul was capable of giving.

13

SURPRISE, SURPRISE!

Karen stepped into her light-filled art studio in the back garden and instantly felt at peace with the world. This was her domain, her little kingdom; this is where inspiration transmogrified into paintings. The intoxicating smell of oil paint and turps enveloped her as she fitted her painting apron over her head and tied it at the back in a loose bow. *Oooh, it's going to be a good painting day today!* she thought, as she ripped the cellophane covering off the new large canvas and placed it on the easel.

After setting out her paints and brushes in neat rows, she picked up her palette and began the underpainting process of a peaceful local scene she had photographed a couple of weeks ago.

The soothing motion of paintbrush gliding over canvas was like a meditation.

It had started about twenty years ago, back in Sydney, when Martin had given her a set of acrylic paints comprised of eight small tubes and a plastic palette, a selection of brushes of varying sizes, and two small canvasses as a present—for no reason other than because he loved her and wanted to give her something. She accepted them happily but had no idea why Martin would give her paints. She had never painted anything more than a wall before, never felt the creative urge, knew nothing about colours, composition, or proportions.

A month or so after he'd given the paints to her, on a cold wintry Sunday when Martin was playing golf and she didn't feel like going out, Karen thought about trying out the paints. Could be a bit of fun....or not!

She set one of the canvasses out on the kitchen counter, placed the little tubes in a nice straight line next to the canvas, the palette next to them, and the brushes across the top. After squeezing a small amount of paint out of one of the tubes onto the palette, she picked up a brush, dipped it into the paint, and swept it across the canvas.

It looked fabulous—a brushstroke of bright, solid yellow on the pure white of the canvas. *Oh, try another colour*, she thought, as she squeezed a little paint from another tube. She cleaned the remaining yellow off the brush with a paper towel and dipped it into a new colour, then applied it to the canvas next to the bright yellow. Fantastic! The new colour was a bright, darkish blue and glistened in the sunlight. This was more fun than she imagined.

She continued to experiment with the rest of the colours. Dark green on the other side of the bright yellow, then the red, the purple, black, white. By the time Karen had used every colour and had covered the canvas, she had created a bright, cheery little abstract.

She had been painting for a couple of hours but hadn't noticed the time; she was having fun.

Creative minds need coffee! She made herself a cup of coffee as she cleaned up the palette and stood the little painting up against the splashback. The kitchen was all white—white cupboards, white tiled splashback, white marble countertop—and the little painting looked spectacular against the white.

She couldn't wait to show it to Martin when he came home from golf. He was husbandly impressed but added, 'Don't give up your day job yet.'

Karen took the little painting into her shop the next day and stood it amongst a display of white kitchen equipment. She attached a price tag of fifty-nine dollars to it. The girls thought it was lovely but didn't think it would sell—who would buy a painting in a kitchenware shop?

Much to everyone's surprise, it sold the following day.

Two days later, Denise approached Karen in the office.

'Karen, we've had two more enquiries about the colourful little painting we had the other day. Don't suppose you could do another one, could you? I told one customer we'd have some more in next week.'

The following Sunday, she experimented on the second canvas using three colours: blue, yellow, and little blobs of white on the blue. *This one looks a bit beachy,* she thought, *but I'll try it out in the shop anyway.*

She took it into the shop the next day and displayed it with the colourful picnic sets, once again priced at fifty-nine dollars. It sold within the week.

Time to buy more canvasses. She kept the paintings the same small size and began to mix some of the colours together, creating two new paintings each Sunday for the next three weeks. Four of the paintings sold quickly, but the other two sat around in the shop for a couple of weeks so Karen removed them from display and kept them in her office.

She examined the two remaining paintings and tried to work out why these ones hadn't sold when the others had practically walked out the door. *Perhaps the colour combinations are wrong,* she thought, *or too much of one and not enough of the other. Maybe it's time to find out a bit more about this painting lark; maybe it's time to take it a bit more seriously.*

The following Sunday, Karen logged onto YouTube and searched 'How to Paint'—and a whole new world opened up to her.

Over the following months, and years, Karen bought many more paints in a multitude of colours; brushes galore—you could never have too many brushes—and various types of palettes from wooden, roundish ones with a hole for your thumb, to large, rectangular Perspex ones, to a pad of disposable sheets. She tried watercolour paint but didn't like it much, then pastels, which she loved. She tried small canvasses, large canvasses, and all sizes in between. What started out as a bit of a hobby took on a life of its own.

Martin being Martin took all the credit for Karen's success with her paintings; after all, it was he who had given her the paints in the first place, all those years ago. Also, it was very handy for birthdays and Christmas—easy to buy a beautiful book on art, or more paints, or a subscription to the Art Gallery of New South Wales.

It was Martin who noticed an article in the Sunday papers about an art workshop in Bathurst, NSW, in a few months' time.

'Karen, have you seen this thing about a week of art workshops being held at Bathurst soon?'

They were having lunch on the balcony in a sunny spot, enjoying Martin's freshly-made scones with home-made raspberry jam and lashings of cream.

'God, these scones are wonderful Martin.' said Karen, as she loaded more jam onto her third scone.

'That's the lemonade. It's Nigella's secret ingredient. They are good, aren't they?' He licked some cream off a finger and reached for another scone as he handed the newspaper section containing the ad to her.

As Karen read the ad, her excitement antennae began to twitch. This looked interesting. The workshop was to run for a week during school holidays in the Bathurst High School, and there would be several artists conducting classes in everything from abstract to life drawing to oil painting to plein air studies. She had never been game enough to try oil paints before, and this would be the perfect opportunity to do it under the guidance of an expert.

She enrolled in the "Oil Painting for Beginners" course.

From the first time Karen used oil paints, all else was left behind. This was the medium for her! The buttery feel of the paint as it smoothed its way onto the canvas, the way the colours stayed true, the way they blended on the canvas. And the smell was intoxicating!

The more she painted, the better her paintings became, more realistic and interesting. Each one told a story. She was never interested in painting commissions; she liked to paint what she wanted to paint, to satisfy herself.

She attended several more workshops conducted by various artists, always enjoyable, always something to learn. She sold a few paintings and had given others to friends and relatives. She didn't paint for other people; she painted to please herself, and the money she received for her paintings wasn't important to her. The joy of having someone appreciate one of her paintings gave her great pleasure.

When they had moved to Coffs Harbour, Karen discovered the Arts and Crafts Community Group there also held some good workshops. Karen enrolled in one coming up on "Painting in Acrylics", which was being run by a famous Australian artist who had a great following and whose paintings Karen admired. She had been painting in oils for several years and thought it was about time she tried acrylics again, especially as acrylic paint had improved considerably in recent years. During a conversation with Lou, he told her the resort had been appointed the principal accommodation for people coming from farther afield or interstate for the workshop. The art teacher would be staying there too. It was going to be a busy time.

Karen arrived early on the first day of the workshop to register. She chatted with the other participants, exchanging names, and views on painting. As she began to unpack her art equipment on one of the long tables, she turned to the woman who was setting up next to her and introduced herself.

'Hi, I'm Karen Cosgrove.' Karen extended her hand, and as the other woman shook hands, she replied, 'Hello Karen, I'm Glenda McElhone.'

Karen stopped breathing for a moment. She brushed her hair back from her face and moved some of her equipment around on the table to give herself some time to recover from the shock. This woman had to be Paul's wife—there couldn't possibly be two Glenda McElhones! She had no idea Paul's wife painted, not that she would have expected him to tell her.

She quickly gained her composure and had a friendly chat with Glenda until the artist-in-charge entered the room and the workshop got underway. The two women developed a 'workshop friendship' over the next few days, chatting amiably, although Karen noticed Glenda never mentioned her husband.

She's quite attractive, thought Karen, when she had a chance to quietly study Glenda. *Speaks with a bit of a lisp—which a lot of men find attractive in a woman. I wonder if he was madly in love with her when they married? I imagine in those days she wouldn't have been able to afford the quality clothes and accessories she's wearing now, which certainly contributes to her overall attractiveness.*

Karen couldn't help wondering what they were like together. Did he find her stimulating company? Was she a good wife to him? At first, it had been quite a shock to meet her, but as the days went by, Karen became intrigued. To accidentally meet your lover's wife was almost funny when she thought about it, like some sort of French farce.

Glenda was effusive about the resort where she was staying, along with several of the others. 'It's really lovely, Karen—nice dining room, great food. You must come and have dinner with us one night.' And then, in a light-bulb moment, added, 'Why don't you come tonight?'

For a split second, Karen thought, *that could be a bit dangerous*. But on second thought, *why not?*

She joined Glenda and a few of the others for dinner and they all had a very enjoyable night—exceptionally good food and top-quality wines. Lou worked Reception that evening and Karen thought he may have been able to arrange a discount for them for dinner, but no luck.

The workshop progressed, and by the end of the week Karen's, and particularly Glenda's, painting skills showed signs of real improvement. Karen realised what she had heard about the improvement in acrylic paint was true.

At this stage, Karen had not let on to Paul she was even doing the workshop—she didn't think he would be interested. She presumed Glenda would mention the people she had met at the workshop when she returned home, but would she mention names? Exactly what information should Karen impart to Paul, if any?

Karen emailed Paul as usual during the following week.

Oh, by the way, I met your wife at a workshop up here last week. Nice painter.

He replied:

Yes, I'd forgotten to mention Glenda was coming up to Coffs to do a workshop. She said she'd met some nice people at the workshop, including you.

Karen then deftly changed the subject, and the workshop wasn't mentioned again.

Workshop over, life returned to normal. Gardening, shopping, painting, cooking. Karen and Martin had Lou over for dinner a couple of weeks later, and Lou told them about the workshop participants who had stayed at the resort. It had been a successful week from the hotel's point of view, and they were going to collaborate with the Arts and Crafts Community Group to arrange more similar workshops in the future. Apparently, painters spend up big on food and alcohol when they get together.

About a month later, Lou rang Karen.

'Hi, Karen, can I ask a favour?' he asked. 'Would you mind feeding Ruffy for a week? I'm going to Sydney to spend some time with the boys. I'd really appreciate it if you could check in on her each day.'

Karen loved Lou's cat, Ruffy, and it was a joy for her to call there each day to feed her and have a cuddle. They had arranged this previously on several occasions and it was no trouble. Lou only lived ten minutes' drive away.

'I'd love to, Lou. You know I love Ruffy. I'd have her over here for the week, but I know she doesn't like her little routine being disturbed.'

As soon as Lou returned home, he rang Karen to thank her for looking after Ruffy. Not long into the conversation, there was a pause and Lou said, 'Um, Karen, I've met a lady, and there's no doubt about it, I'm smitten. She's different to the others. She's a bit of a free spirit and we seem to get on well together. She lives a fair way away so it's not like I'm seeing her every day, but we've met up a couple of times now and have really enjoyed each other's company. I think she feels the same way.'

Karen was delighted for him; he had not talked so enthusiastically about anyone he had met previously, and she hoped this time it might be serious.

'Lou, that's great news. I'm happy for you. What's her name?'

'I'd rather not tell you her name yet in case it doesn't last. She's married, but apparently, it's not a happy marriage. From what she's told me, he's a bully and is aggressive and controlling. He's not just verbally abusive—he's even threatened her physically a couple of times. She's planning on leaving him when the time is right.'

'Be careful, Lou. It's never a good idea to get involved in anyone else's marriage. I mean, she may know what she's doing, but don't let her drag you into her situation.'

'I hear what you say, Karen, and that's why I don't want to tell you too much about her in case it all blows up and gets unpleasant. But I do want to be there for her if and when she leaves him.'

'That's very decent of you, Lou. I'm delighted you've met someone you care about, and I'm always here if you ever want to talk it out.'

Karen could understand why this woman would be attracted to Lou. He was such a gentle and kind person, but she also hoped he wasn't being used.

When Lou asked Karen if she would take care of Ruffy on a couple of other occasions, she smiled to herself and thought, *I bet he's going away with Lady X. I sure hope so!*

Eventually, Lou phoned Karen to tell her he'd invited his lady friend to come and stay with him in Coffs for a few days. Karen was genuinely delighted. 'Oh, Lou, this is terrific news. Why don't you bring her over for dinner one night while she's here? We'd love to meet her.'

Karen was quietly excited about meeting Lou's lady friend. She asked Martin if he would do something special for dinner, perhaps a nice crown roast rather than a barbecue, and maybe a celebratory desert—this would be a special occasion! And, of course, champagne.

It started to rain, heavily, about an hour before Lou and his friend were due to arrive, no lightning yet but a bit of thunder, so it was a good thing they had decided against a barbecue outside. The table setting Karen arranged in the dining room looked informal even though the wineglasses sparkled and the newly polished cutlery shone brilliantly. Although she didn't want to intimidate Lou's lady friend, Karen loved using her best table linen and silverware, and the mouth-watering aroma of the dinner roasting in the oven added to the ambiance. She mulled over what to wear for an hour or so before deciding on the new navy slacks and cream sweater she'd bought yesterday.

She heard Lou's car pull up in the drive and waited for him to ring the doorbell. Glancing quickly in the hall mirror as she passed it, she tucked a stray strand of hair behind her ear, and opened the front door, smiling.

And there stood Lou...and Glenda!!

14

THE DINNER

Shit!

I thought for a second that was Glenda.

Oh shit!

It IS Glenda.

Thoughts raced through Karen's mind in the second or two it took for her to breathe out.

Just say the words: 'Glenda, nice to see you again.'

Say the words. Say the words.

SPEAK!!!!

'Glenda, how nice to see you again! And what a surprise. Hi Lou, come in, come in.'

Karen ushered them both out of the dark rainy night into the warm, welcoming house, while her mind continued to race, a mire of confusion and secrets.

At this stage, Lou was looking a bit sheepish, but beaming at the same time. 'I wanted to tell you it was Glenda, but I really wanted it to be a surprise. The look on your face when you saw her was worth a thousand words. The surprise part was better than I expected.' And both he and Glenda looked at each other and laughed.

Karen smiled to hide the turmoil going on in her head. As she took their coats and made a fuss of hanging them on the hooks in the entry foyer, she called to Martin, 'Martin, we've got visitors. Can you stop whatever you're doing and come and say hello?'

On his way into the living room, Martin picked up the bottle of champagne and four glasses.

'Hello Lou, good to see you. And who do we have here?'

Lou made the introductions as Martin put the glasses and bottle on the coffee table and shook hands with each of them. 'Well, this calls for champagne all round,' he said, and then added, after a very brief pause, 'You do drink champagne, don't you, Glenda?'

'Absolutely! I am so pleased to meet you both. Lou has told me all about you and how he first met Karen when she had her kitchenware shop.'

Karen tried to quell the panic inside while they were making small talk, wracking her brain, trying to remember if she had mentioned Glenda to Martin at the time of the painting workshop, wondering what the best way was to handle this situation that had caught her so off guard. What would be the repercussions of this relationship between Lou and Glenda as far as Paul was concerned, especially after Glenda told him she was leaving him?

And then the worst-case scenario exploded like a bomb in her mind—it would be disastrous if Paul ever found out Glenda had been to Karen's place for dinner.

Months ago, when Karen had asked Lou the lady's name and he had preferred not to tell, Glenda would have been the very last name she would have guessed. But of course, now she knew, she remembered the times Lou went to Sydney to 'see his family'—Glenda must have come up to Sydney to be with him. Karen wondered how she had managed to get away on her own. What excuse had she used? According to Paul, Glenda occasionally went on a shopping trip for a day or two with girlfriends, but as far as she knew, it didn't happen very often.

Like the first bolt of lightning that precedes an approaching storm, Karen remembered what Paul had told her about his wife having mental health issues and how she often lied and exaggerated. Lou had said Glenda's husband was aggressive, controlling, abusive, and that she was leaving him. Judging by what she knew of Paul, and from what he had told her, this was all lies. One thing was definite—Paul was not aggressive, controlling, or abusive, and to imagine him being physically violent was laughable.

Obviously, Lou knew nothing of this side of Glenda. He was in love with the woman and believed she was going to leave her husband to be with him. And because Karen's relationship with Paul was secret, she couldn't let on to Lou that he was involved with a very troubled woman. But how could she let her friend continue a relationship based on lies and fantasy? Karen doubted Glenda would ever leave Paul—it would mean she would have to deal with reality.

As the dinner progressed, Karen managed to maintain a steady stream of small talk, and, of course, Martin's meal was really something. He excelled himself with the perfect standing roast, although Karen found each mouthful difficult to swallow. When everyone had finished the first course, she cleared away the plates and suggested Martin open the bottle of white wine Lou had brought with him.

'And tell me, Martin, what treat do you have in store for us for dessert?' Lou asked as he sampled the wine.

'Yes, Martin, I can't wait to hear what's next,' Glenda said. 'Lou told me you were a wonderful cook, but I must say, I didn't expect anything as special as that roast. It was better than any restaurant I've ever been to. Almost as good as something Lou has cooked for me.' She smiled coyly at Lou, who winked at her and squeezed her hand under the table.

'Well, I thought I'd try something I recently came across in an old recipe book of Karen's,' Martin replied. 'It's called Orange Blossom Delizia. Never done it before—have no idea what it'll be like, but it sounds magnificent! It's like tiramisu, but it's made with marmalade and Cointreau, and lots of chocolate curls.'

'Bring it on,' said Lou, and he and Glenda glanced at each other and laughed.

Lou poured the wine for Glenda, and Karen noticed he didn't pour another one for himself. He'd had one glass of champagne and one glass of wine—no more for him this evening. Lou was always careful about drinking and driving, even though it was only a short drive to his place.

Glenda, on the other hand, didn't hold back. She was a great raconteur and had them laughing as she told some amazing stories about when she worked as a receptionist for a funeral director (*probably all made up*, thought Karen). The stories became more varied and outrageous the more wine she drank although Karen noticed she was in control enough to avoid any mention of her husband or son.

Lou was having the time of his life. Karen hadn't seen him this happy for many years. His good friends had taken to Glenda and he couldn't stop smiling. It warmed her heart to think her friend had found happiness at last, but the warmth was undermined by a feeling of trepidation and apprehension.

Eventually, it was time for them to leave. Martin and Karen walked them to the front door and Martin helped Glenda on with her coat since she didn't seem capable of doing it herself.

'Oh, thank you, Martin. I don't seem to know my right arm from my left. Didn't think I'd ever find the correct sleeve,' she said, giggling and twirling as she wrapped the coat around her.

The sensor light outside came on as Karen opened the front door. Still raining. A dark, cold, very wet night. The strain of the evening was beginning to tell on Karen and she wanted them gone.

'Lovely meeting you, Glenda,' Martin said as he waved them off. 'We look forward to doing this again.'

Oh, for God's sake, Martin, shut up, Karen thought as she kissed Lou on the cheek and said, ''Night, Lou. Drive carefully.'

As the visitors drove off into the night, Martin and Karen closed the door and Karen let out a sigh. *Thank God that's over,* she thought. She'd got through the evening without a slipup, but it had been a Herculean effort.

Together, Karen and Martin cleared away the dinner things and Martin put the dishwasher on as Karen tidied the table. By the time they went upstairs to bed, nobody would have known they'd had guests for dinner.

Martin fell into bed exhausted but pleased with himself. 'That went well, don't you think? She seems rather lovely, and he's mad about her,' he said as he switched off the bedside lamp.

'Wonderful,' muttered Karen, rolling her eyes as she stretched out in bed and tried to calm her busy mind. When she glanced over at Martin, he was already fast asleep and gently snoring.

But Karen could not grasp the velvety black abyss of peaceful sleep she so desperately wanted. The 'chattering monkeys' in her head would not go away as her mind analysed and dissected everything said during the evening.

Eventually, about an hour later, after tossing and turning and worried she might wake Martin, she slid out of bed and crept downstairs to make a cup of tea. She had just switched the kettle on when her phone rang. It was Lou.

In a shaky, crackly voice, unlike anything she'd heard before, he said, 'Karen, we've been in a terrible accident. We're in hospital. I'm okay, but Glenda is badly injured.'

'Oh God, Lou, how awful. I'll come to the hospital now. Give me a few minutes to get dressed.'

Close to panic, Karen raced upstairs and changed into jeans and a sweater. Martin was dead to the world and snoring loudly, so she scribbled a quick note to let him know what had happened, should he wake before she got back. With racing heart and mind, she quickly backed the car out of the garage and drove as fast, but as carefully, as she could to the hospital.

The situation could not have been worse, for all concerned. But then, she didn't know how bad things could get.

Karen parked in the hospital car park and ran through the rain into the hospital. She was breathless when she finally located Lou in a room on the fourth floor.

He was lying on the bed, wearing a white hospital gown with a drip needle in his arm. Other than that, he didn't look too bad, although he was very pale. The only sign of injury she could see was the strapping on his forearm and a smallish plaster on his forehead.

'How are you?' Karen asked immediately on entering the room, gasped for breath and holding her chest. Her legs were shaking from running and she flopped down in the visitor's chair next to the bed. She reached out and took hold of Lou's hand. 'God, what happened, Lou? How is Glenda? You said she was badly injured.' The words spilled out of Karen's mouth as she tried to get her breath back.

'Oh, Karen. I'm so glad you're here. It was a terrible accident. I can't get the noise of the crash out of my head; I keep hearing it every time I close my eyes.'

'A car coming from the opposite direction swerved across in front of us, almost as if he was turning, but I think he hit an oil patch on the road. I swerved to try and avoid him, but the front passenger side of my car hit the front passenger side of his car. I hit the brakes and slowed the car enough so when we crossed onto the wrong side of the road and down the embankment, the car stopped in a ditch, but by then, the damage was done. Glenda copped the full impact.'

By now, Lou was distraught and clutching Karen's hand tightly. 'After the first impact, the other driver completely lost control of his car on the wet road and slammed into a tree. Oh, Karen, the sound of the impact was incredible. Apparently, his left leg was crushed but, Karen, the woman in the front passenger seat of the car was killed on impact.' All colour had drained from Lou's face, and he was taking huge gulps of air, trying to calm the panic he felt.

Karen stood up and almost fell onto the bed, still gripping Lou's hand. She suddenly felt very old, and sick to her stomach, her heart pounding in her chest. Her breathing became erratic and her mouth felt dry and distasteful.

'Oh God, what a dreadful thing to happen,' she said. 'The poor driver. Had he been drinking, do you know?'

'I don't think so,' he said. 'The police arrived the same time as the ambulance and they took blood samples from everyone involved for alcohol testing, but apparently, both drivers' came back negative. I was able to get 000 on my phone and they got to us quickly, but I could hear the paramedics talking as they got Glenda and me into the ambulance. They said they needed to get her to the hospital quickly in order to save her leg. The nurse here was the one who told me the passenger in the other car was dead when the ambulance arrived. I think Glenda's leg was also crushed. I don't even know if they could save it. They don't tell you much.' He looked down. 'I've got a gash on my forearm and I'm probably in shock. Plus, I've got a killer headache. They're sending me down for X-rays shortly.'

Karen's breathing had slowed, and she no longer thought she might throw up. 'If you're okay for the moment, I'll go and try and find out how Glenda is.'

The Nurses' Station was close by Lou's room, and Karen asked one of the doctors there if he could tell her how Glenda McElhone was.

'I've just come from Mrs. McElhone. She's currently in an induced coma and we've made her as comfortable as possible. Are you family?' asked the doctor.

'No. Why do you ask?' Karen's mind raced ahead. *Why would the doctor want to know if I was family?*

'She can't have any visitors other than family yet.'

'Has her family been notified?' asked Karen, trying to make it sound like a reasonable question, while she was silently screaming inside her head.

'I think the police are taking care of that.'

Oh God, poor Paul...getting a phone call from the police in another state, in the middle of the night.

There was nothing more she could do or say, and she found her way back to Lou's room. She managed to avoid bumping into a doctor as he was coming out of the doorway.

'Ah, Mrs. Cosgrove. Lou told me you're his close friend and you'll be able to come and pick him up tomorrow if he's okay to be discharged.'

'Yes. Is he going to be all right?' *Physically, at least. Emotionally, this is a disaster.*

The doctor smiled benignly. 'I'm sure he'll be fine. The X-rays are just to make sure there's no damage we can't see.

He should be ready to go home around lunchtime tomorrow.' And he continued on his way.

'Were you able to find out how Glenda is?' Lou asked anxiously. He looked pale and tired and it was an effort for him to speak.

'She's resting now. They'll know more tomorrow when they've done some tests,' Karen lied. 'I'll go now and let you get some rest. Why don't you ring me when you're ready to be discharged and I'll come and pick you up? Maybe you should come and stay with us for a few days.'

A look of resistance to this suggestion crossed Lou's face.

'Lou, it will be easier than me calling over to your place every day to make sure you're not overdoing it.'

'Okay. You're probably right. I'll ring you when they decide to discharge me.'

'Good night, Lou. I hope you can get some sleep. See you soon,' Karen said as she kissed him on the cheek and left.

What a predicament, thought Karen as she carefully drove home. *Poor Lou. He must be so worried. Poor Glenda; she doesn't even know the extent of her injuries. And poor Paul...he'll be so confused when the police contact him with news of his wife's accident, so far from home. And what am I going to do? How am I going to handle this?*

Karen parked the car in the garage and quietly slipped upstairs. She tossed the note she had written earlier in the wastepaper basket, undressed, and climbed back into bed beside a snoring Martin. She lay awake for the next hour or so, her mind working at a hundred miles an hour before sleep eventually overcame her. She slept fitfully for a few hours until she woke with a start about eight o'clock. Martin wasn't beside her!

Wrapping her gown around her, she hurried downstairs and found him enjoying a leisurely breakfast and reading the newspaper.

Martin looked up from his newspaper and smiled. 'Oh, good morning, darling. How are you this morning? I got the impression you didn't sleep very well.' As he spoke, he noticed Karen looked rather dishevelled. She still had her makeup on from last night and her eyes looked weary and dark.

'I'm afraid I have some bad news,' she said. 'Lou and Glenda were involved in a car accident on the way home last night.'

Martin put the newspaper down immediately. He looked stricken. No matter what the situation, Martin always expected the worst. 'What happened?'

'I was in the kitchen making myself a cup of tea because I couldn't sleep when Lou rang to say they were both in hospital following an accident. I didn't want to wake you, so I drove to the hospital to see what the situation was. Lou's injuries were superficial, but Glenda was more seriously injured.'

Karen relayed to Martin what Lou had told her of the crash, but he could see she was more intent on their injuries.

'Lou has a cut on his arm and his forehead, and a severe headache,' she went on. 'But other than that, he seems to be okay. They're taking some X-rays this morning and then hopefully, he'll be discharged from hospital. However, I think Glenda's leg was crushed in the accident. I do hope she's going to be okay. Lou's going to ring me when he's discharged, and I'll go and pick him up. I'll bring him back here for a few days.'

'Good idea. I'll come with you,' Martin said, and Karen flinched internally. The last thing she needed was for Martin to come to the hospital with her.

He continued: 'Gee, I hope Glenda is going to be okay. She seemed such a nice person. I don't know her circumstances, but I thought she and Lou got on so well together. Has he told you much about her? Do you think their relationship is serious?'

'I don't know much about her at all, except Lou seems to be really fond of her,' she answered. 'I hope for his sake she's going to be okay, although a crushed leg sounds bad. I'm sure we'll find out more about it later.'

Karen busied herself making a cup of tea as Martin got back to his newspaper and toast. She took her tea out onto the terrace; she needed to physically distance herself from Martin to avoid any further conversation about Glenda.

It was around lunchtime when Lou texted Karen to let her know he was going to be discharged in about an hour.

As Karen and Martin were preparing to leave the house, their next-door neighbour, a rather timid, elderly lady, rushed up the driveway in a panic. Karen noticed her hands were shaking and she looked upset, as if she might burst into tears any minute.

'Oh, Karen. Missy has eaten some snail pellets. They're poisonous and I've got to get her to the vet quickly. I'm sorry to ask you at such short notice, but would it be possible for one of you to drive us to the vet?'

She was in quite a state and Karen thought to herself, *it must be awful when you're elderly and live alone and something happens to your beloved pet.*

'Of course. Martin can drive you and Missy to the vet, Alma.' Karen placed a reassured hand on Alma's arm. Then, turning to Martin, she added with what she hoped was a convincing smile, 'It's really not necessary for you to come with me, Martin. Better for you to take Alma straight to the vet's. I'll see you back here later.' Karen desperately hoped the much-loved cat would be okay, but she was relieved to be able to go to the hospital alone.

To get to the hospital by the most direct route, Karen had to drive along the road where the accident had happened. The two badly smashed vehicles looked like they were in the same position as when the crash occurred, and a police car was parked on the side of the road. Two policemen were taking measurements and surveying the area, while another man was photographing the area from various angles. The scene disturbed Karen and she couldn't help thinking of the passenger in the other car and the loved-ones who would never see her again. The tragedy of it seemed even more gut-wrenching today as the sun shone in a clear bright blue sky, the roads completely dry and fresh looking after last night's rain.

As she entered the hospital and proceeded to Lou's room, Karen passed an open door to a room on the ground floor. She glanced in and saw two uniformed policemen talking to a man whom she recognized with a start as a distraught-looking Paul. She caught her breath in her throat and stumbled in fright, but she was sure he hadn't seen her as she hurried on her way to Lou's room, her mind awash with thoughts of how best to handle the situation.

Lou was dressed and sitting on the bed looking pale and fragile when Karen entered. He seemed to be shivering. He looked up at her, and she saw the tears well in his eyes, as he exclaimed, 'Oh, Karen, have you heard? Glenda died about an hour ago.'

15

A DAGGER TO THE HEART

Karen slumped down on the bed beside him in shock, trying not to show how stunned she was by this revelation. Her heart pounded in her ears, and she suddenly felt hot and faint. Her first thought was for Paul. *He must be distraught. Did he see her before she died? How long had he been here at the hospital?*

She felt beads of sweat break out on her forehead, the palms of her hands instantly clammy and sticky. 'Lou, I'm so sorry. I thought she was going to be okay. I knew they would only allow family to visit her, but I never for a moment thought she was so badly injured. What a terrible thing to happen to a woman in the prime of her life, with so much to live for. Do you know what happened?'

Lou's breath caught in his throat and he rubbed both fists into his eyes as if the rubbing would ease his sadness. 'The RN on this floor came and told me about a half hour ago that Glenda had died as a result of the accident. She said a break in a major bone like the femur bone can be dangerous, as it can cause a person to bleed out. Apparently, she lost a great deal of blood.' He paused. 'I can't believe this happened. We had such a good evening last night, the four of us. I remember feeling so happy as we were driving home. I can't believe she's gone.'

As Lou was speaking, a cloud passed over the sun and the room became dim and gloomy, which exacerbated the sad atmosphere. The room swam before Karen's eyes and, for the second time, she thought she would faint. She wrapped her arms around Lou, as much to steady her shaking hands as to comfort him. This dear man, this dear friend, should not have to endure another tragedy surrounding the women in his life. Just when it seemed like he had found some genuine happiness at last, it had been snatched away from him.

Karen had never felt confident about this woman who had entered Lou's life, had never truly believed she would 'leave her husband to be with Lou,' but she had never thought for one moment it would end in tragedy. She wanted so badly for him to be happy.

At that moment, the young doctor she had passed in the corridor entered the room. He looked at Karen and said, 'Would you mind giving us a few minutes? We have to do some final checks before we can discharge Mr. Bristow. If you can call back here in about fifteen minutes, he should be ready to go.'

As she walked along the corridor, Karen shook her head to clear her thoughts, but the knot in her stomach only tightened. A dark and foreboding feeling enveloped her. Slightly dazed and unable to take everything in, she came to the room in which she had seen the policemen talking to Paul earlier.

The two policemen were walking out of the room when one of them turned back to face Paul and she overhead him saying, 'We'll submit our report on the accident, and your wife's body will be transported to Newcastle for the inquest. You'll be kept informed.'

They left, and as Karen glanced inside, she saw Paul sitting, slumped forward in a chair, his elbows on his knees, his head in his hands. What began as a bad dream had deteriorated into a nightmare and was spiralling out of control. The situation was now far worse than she could ever have imagined.

Standing there, wondering what to do, Karen made a split-second decision and entered the room. Paul glanced up when he heard her footsteps and immediately stood. Karen rushed to him, put her hand on his arm, and looked into his eyes. 'Oh, Paul, I am so sorry. So deeply sorry.'

Before she could say another word, Paul wheeled around and shook her hand off. He took a step back. 'Don't touch me. Don't come near me.'

Karen recoiled in surprise.

'My wife is dead,' he said. 'Do you understand? My wife is dead. The police investigating the accident said Glenda and the man driving the car had dinner at your house last night. How could you invite her to dinner at your house? Your house!! You knew she was my wife. How could you? How could you betray me? How could you conspire against me like that?'

His voice had grown louder and more distraught with each word until he was almost shouting. Karen struggled to find the right words to say, to try and soothe the hurt, but instead, a feeling of disbelief and shame threatened to overwhelm her.

Again: 'How could you betray me like that?'

He paused and took a sobbing breath, his shaking fingers massaging his forehead in confusion. He breathed out audibly, then spoke quietly and with such feeling Karen felt her heart crack in her chest. 'I loved you, Karen. I loved you more than I've ever loved another person.' He looked like a little lost boy, teary and bewildered, as he shook his head in disbelief. 'I trusted you, and you betrayed me.'

I loved you, Karen. I loved you more than I've ever loved another person. The words obliterated all else in her head, repeating over and over in her mind. *I loved you, Karen. I loved you more than I've ever loved another person.* And then, suddenly, another thought: *Why did you never say that, Paul? Why did you never tell me? Why did you never tell me you loved me?*

Love. Only a small word, but one whose meaning was so big, so huge, Karen thought she would buckle under its weight. How could such a small word carry such an impact? Why did it have such power? Why did it touch hearts, move heaven and earth? Cause people to do weird and often wonderful things. Affect so deeply?

Karen felt like she'd been smashed in the chest with a steel rod. *Why did you never say that to me? Why did you never let the word pass your lips—until now?*

'But, Paul, I knew nothing about—'

'Stop! Stop.' He was speaking very quietly now, in shock and anger. He thrust his hand out, creating a barrier between the two of them. 'Don't say another word.' And then the words she never wanted to hear: 'I never want to see you again. I never want to hear from you again. Do not ever contact me again.'

The nurse who entered the room must have heard the last few words, but Paul looked at her and said calmly and coldly, 'Mrs. Cosgrove is leaving. Could you please show her the way out?'

The nurse looked slightly confused. She could feel the tension in the room, the heat emanating from these two people. With a worried look on her face, she turned to Karen. 'This way, Mrs. Cosgrove,' and led her out into the corridor.

Karen stumbled back toward Lou's room, her mind in turmoil. Oh God. Oh God, this was worse than she had expected. Her world was crumbling around her and she was powerless to stop it.

And still his words continued to swirl in her head: *I loved you, Karen. I loved you more than I've ever loved another person.*

She felt helpless and hopeless. Her world had moved on its axis and there was nothing she could do to right it.

16

SOCIETY'S RULES

Winter melted into spring, and suddenly it was summer, in all its glory—hot, sunburnt days and warm, humid nights, the occasional summer thunderstorm, and torrential rain.

And still, the darkness in Karen's heart didn't fade into light. She still grieved for the loss of Paul and their relationship, still missed their intimate conversations, the wonderful sex, the mental and physical stimulation he provided each time they met. Her life lacked that joie de vivre, the anticipation of the next email, the next chat, the next getaway together. The days seemed longer, duller, less joyful, and the often-sleepless nights seemed to go on forever. She would give anything to one day open her email account and see his name in her inbox. But as the days dissolved into weeks, then months, she realised that was never going to happen.

Lou recovered well from his physical injuries; no outward signs, no scars, the headache at last completely gone. But Karen didn't think he would ever completely recover emotionally or spiritually. The re-ignited light in his life had gone out the day Glenda died.

Karen sat at her computer composing yet another email to Paul.

My dearest Paul, please tell me if there is anything I can do or say to make you understand. Tell me what I can say to convince you ....

Delete, delete, delete.

Email number seventeen—which would never be sent, like all the others.

Crash went the side door as Martin strode into the house from the garage, arms full of groceries.

'Hello, darling, I'm home,' he called out. 'I'll do a deal with you—I'll put the shopping away if you'll make a cup of tea for us.'

I suppose anything is better than putting away the groceries, thought Karen as she walked into the kitchen and filled the kettle. *But one of these days, I'm going to scream when he says that. Scream and throw something.*

'Did you remember Lou is coming for dinner tonight? I bought some lamb chops to barbecue with maybe the special Thai sauce I make—you know, the hot one Lou likes. What do you think?'

'Sounds lovely, Martin. Lou will like that.'

Dear Lou. Dear Lou, who had learned to mask his true feelings behind a happy face when Martin was around. Oh, Martin felt sorry for Lou, and even made an effort to say and do the right thing as far as Lou was concerned, but he really wished Lou would 'get over it' so they could all move on to the life they enjoyed before 'the terrible accident.'

With the table set for dinner and nothing else needing to be done, Karen sat enjoying a gin and tonic in the big comfy armchair, looking out over the garden at the red ball of setting sun as it gently descended to greet the dark evening horizon.

She loved this time of the day, especially when she was alone in the house. Martin was out watering the garden, and Lou wasn't due for another half an hour at least. This was her thinking time, her inner meditation time.

Karen sipped her drink and let her mind wander, slipping and sliding over events, emotions, memories. Inevitably, she began to think about the people in her life, past and present, and how life has a way of getting even, of showing us there's a price to pay for breaking society's rules.

Lou, a single man of good moral values, a widower who was free of the responsibilities of family life, footloose and available. But he broke society's rules and formed a relationship with a woman he knew to be married and eventually lost her in the worst possible way.

Glenda, married to a man who was himself unfaithful, but who also broke society's rules and lied and cheated in order to become involved with another man. She had paid for her infidelity with her life, as a result of being with her lover in the wrong place, at the wrong time.

Paul, a married man, who broke society's rules and began an affair with a married woman, who 'never planned on getting caught,' but who ended up alone and broken following the tragic death of his wife.

Then there was Karen herself, a married woman who should have known better, who broke society's rules and became entrenched in an affair with a married man. She was deeply and irrevocably hurt when the affair ended, when her lover told her he didn't ever want to see her again.

And Martin, blissfully innocent, and ignorant, of this web of deceit and lies, continued to live a self-absorbed and egocentric life completely unaware of the consequences for the other players in this complicated human catastrophe called life.

17

AND SO IT GOES...

Karen sat in the big armchair looking out on the garden, drinking coffee and nibbling the last piece of Christmas cake. *Thank God Christmas and the whole New Year thing is over, and we can get back to our normal routines.*

She had never liked Christmas ever since Tony was little and Martin insisted on buying him far too many toys. As the years went by, the gifts he bought for Tony became more and more expensive and lavish, and Tony had less and less need or desire for them. But still Martin insisted. Nothing was too good for Tony. Over time, Karen had grown to hate this materialistic aspect of Christmas and even the actual day itself.

Probably by a type of osmosis, Tony had absorbed his mother's dislike for the holiday season many years ago. As soon as he obtained his degree, he spent a year travelling around Europe. Martin was despondent at first—he missed Tony very much, but he was mortified when Tony decided to stay and make a life in the UK, where he still lived.

Karen sat watching the rain fall, saturating the desperately dry lawn, soaking into the garden beds. You could almost hear the weeds grow. Martin had gone to the Golf Club to have a few drinks with his mates as it was too wet to play golf, and she was alone in the house. It had been raining, not hard, but continually, for the past two days, and Karen was getting tired of it now. Funny how a few days of rain made her restless.

She finished the last bite of the cake and drained her coffee cup, stood and stretched her legs, and began to roam around the house.

Wandering into her office, she sat down at the computer and tapped a few keys. *Might as well see if I've got any new emails. Check Facebook*

Then, as she sat staring at the screen, a thought crawled slowly and insidiously across her mind, like a spider on a wall, slowly making his way toward an unknowing prey.

I wonder if Jeff would remember me. I wonder if he'd reply if I emailed him. It would be nice to hear from him again, read one of his long and interesting emails. I miss his correspondence.

Tap, tap, tap.

Hi Jeff, I don't know if you remember me, from http://www.letsbefriends.com.

We emailed each other last year for quite a while.

I was just sitting here at my computer wondering how you are and how life is treating you? I've missed you.....

AUTHOR'S NOTES

Thank you for reading this book. There's a lot of choice out there and every time you, the reader, decide to read a book, it's a commitment of both faith and time. I'm a reader too, I understand.

I hope 'The Life and Loves of Karen Romano' didn't disappoint. If you enjoyed it, I'd be grateful if you could leave a short review, perhaps on Amazon or Goodreads. It helps so much. I have no hope of matching the marketing budgets of the large publishers, and a good review really does make a difference. I do read them all, I promise.

There are bits and pieces of true stories in 'The Life, and Loves, of Karen Romano', people I have known or met along life's path. But mainly, it's a work of fiction.

If you have any questions or comments, I'd love to hear from you. Feel free to email me at:

raynette@raynettemitchellauthor.com

ACKNOWLEDGEMENTS

Every endeavour involves many people—writing a book is no different. The thing I like about researching, writing, and publishing a book is that you meet and speak to so many people, some of whom are known to you and some you've never met before—in fact, many more than I could list here. Their valued time and knowledge is much appreciated on this long and winding road. Without their help and support, this book would have ended up in the rubbish bin long ago, but instead, here it is with its shiny new cover and pristine printing and binding.

To the members of my writers' group—Jacki, Jeremy, Paul, and Trevor—I am forever grateful. Thank you also to my ever-helpful team of beta readers whose feedback and advice made the book better—Carolyn, Cindy, Deborah, Elaine, Heather, Jan, Lee, Lesley, Lorraine, and the wonderful Whitney.

Thank you to the courteous and helpful police men and women at the Prahran Police Station, Victoria, for answering my many questions about shop-lifting charges and traffic accidents. They never once let on that I was a nuisance.

To the administration staff at the faculties of Science and Architecture at Melbourne University, Victoria, who at first couldn't understand why anyone would want to know about their courses 40 years ago, but who went to no end of trouble to find out for me anyway, thank you.

And thanks to the Administrator of the Frank Lloyd Wright Foundation who made Taliesin West, Frank Lloyd Wright's magnificent winter home in Arizona, USA, come alive for me.

And of course, last and most, my long-suffering husband. Dearest Basil, I couldn't have done it without you. Thank you sincerely for your support and encouragement, especially when I needed it the most.

AUTHOR BIO

Raynette Mitchell is an Australian author of contemporary literary fiction who enjoys writing about the complexities of the human condition, and how people handle life situations in good times and in bad.

After countless re-writes and edits, she completed her first book. Her second novel followed quickly so she decided to make it a series of three, under the sub-title of "Secrets Have Consequences". The third book in the series will be released in 2025.

Some of her favourite authors are Marian Keyes, Jodi Picoult, and Joy Dettman. However, she also enjoys reading classics by some of the renowned authors of our time - Winston Graham, John Irving, Ken Follett, John O'Hara, Guy Bellamy.

When she's not writing, Raynette thinks about writing, talks about writing, discusses writing with other authors, and sometimes occasionally even spends a bit of time gardening. Her husband has been a great help in all these endeavours, especially the gardening.

AND COMING UP NEXT.....

If you enjoyed The Life and Loves of Karen Romano, you're going to love the next book in the Secrets Have Consequences series.

The following is the first chapter of **THE LIFE, AND TIMES, OF TOM WATSON**, due out early 2025:

Read on.......

PALO ALTO, CALIFORNIA, 1977

Jim Watson's first reaction, when he was summoned to the office of the Vice-President of the hugely successful IT company he worked for, was impending doom. There had been a spate of redundancies in middle management lately and he presumed the worst.

He took a deep breath as he patted down a stray wisp of hair on the crown of his head and, with chin up, affected his most managerial face as the secretary ushered him into the VP's superbly appointed office

'Sit down, Jim. I've got a proposition for you.' Jim sat, somewhat relieved—this was not usually how a redundancy notice was handled.

'We're putting the finishing touches to a new custom-built office and warehouse complex in Sydney, Australia. It will be an important part of our Asian operations, and I'm looking for someone to organise the move and run the division for a year or two.'

'I'd like to offer you the job. It's a big step up from your current position of Divisional Manager, but I believe you'll handle the added responsibility well. And of course, it comes with a commensurate salary and benefits. What do you say?'

Jim relaxed and replied, 'I've heard rumours about the new complex being built in Sydney. I believe it'll comprise the latest in warehousing and distribution, with office organisation even beyond what we've got here.'

He smiled as he stood and extended his hand across the desk. 'I accept.'

Jim was not only chuffed with the promotion and the financial benefits it brought with it, but he was also excited by the prospect of living in Sydney, Australia. He had visited Australia several times and had enjoyed the atmosphere and living conditions there, which were the best in the world. He thought his son, Tom, would be happy about the move.

But he had doubts about his mother, Enid's, reaction. It would be a huge upheaval for a woman of her age to move to another country, away from her friends, and the support group which had formed around her following the death of her beloved husband six years ago.

Enid had moved in with Jim and Tom three years ago when Jim's wife, Carolyn, was killed in an accident. Tom had been eight at the time and had been badly affected by his mother's death. His grief was ongoing—until his Gran gave him a guitar for his ninth birthday after talking with Mr. O'Brien, the music teacher at Tom's school, who had told her Tom was exceptionally talented and should be encouraged.

Since moving in with them, Enid had reared Tom as her own and had been a steadying influence in his young life. Her age and wisdom meant she was aware of what 9, 10, 11-year-old-boys get up to and Tom had been guided through these years with a firm and knowing hand. He was a good boy, but any boy growing up through those formative years without a mother could have easily been led the wrong way. Enid's experience and intelligence had ensured Tom learned life's lessons without too much heartache and angst.

As Jim drove his now twelve-year-old son to his guitar lesson the following day, he glanced across at Tom and said casually, 'I've been offered a promotion with HP in Sydney, which means we would have to move to Sydney for a year or perhaps two. What would you say to living in Australia for a while?'

This question caught Tom by surprise. He'd heard of Australia and he knew Sydney was the biggest city in that country. He also knew Australia had some deadly reptiles and insects and Kangaroos but that was as much as he knew. It wasn't as if he had many close friends here he would miss, but music had become a large part of his life and he would miss his music teacher, Mr. O'Brien. He rubbed the left side of his face with his open hand as he thought for a long moment before replying, 'Sounds OK. Will Gran come with us?'

'I haven't mentioned it to her yet. Let's tell her about it at dinner tonight.'

The conversation over dinner was difficult. Jim Watson had worked hard for this promotion at Hewlett Packard and the transfer to Australia was a reward for his management skills and loyalty to the firm. He wanted this promotion, but at the same time, he wanted his son and mother to be happy about the move.

When Jim set out the prospect and what it entailed, he could tell Enid was surprised and disappointed.

Enid took a deep breath and regained her composure before she spoke.

'The opportunity of living in another country for a few years is one any 12-year-old-boy should grab with both hands,' she said, taking hold of Tom's hands and smiling into his eyes. 'What an experience! You'll learn about a new and different place to what has been your comfort zone for 12 years. You'll make new friends, hear different voices, taste fresh foods, and discover another culture. Oh, Tom, it will be the making of you.'

Jim shifted slightly in his chair, his heart full of gratitude for this wonderful, wise woman and the words she had chosen. He watched Tom intently for his reaction.

'Do you think so, Gran?' Tom smiled shyly. 'I thought it sounded like fun. Will you come with us?'

'I'm a bit old to take on a new country, so I won't come with you to Australia. But imagine what fun it will be when we get together at Thanksgiving and Christmas? There'll be so much to catch up on; it'll be like a month-long party.'

So, Jim had his answer. He let out the breath he had been holding and said, 'It'll just be you and me looking out for each other, Tom. Do you reckon we can make a go of it?'

'I read somewhere there are some good guitarists in Australia. It would be great if we could get to see some of them.' He looked at his father expectantly.

So much for looking out for each other, thought Jim. *I'll fade into the background in no time at all.* He smiled and tousled his son's hair. 'So, it's agreed. Gran will stay and look after this house and you and I will go on a big adventure to Australia. They'll wonder what hit them when we get there!'

Jim and Tom bustled down the aisle of the plane, shuffling and struggling with their hand luggage between the rows of seats as all the passengers tried to get off it as quickly as possible. As Tom reached the Exit door and stepped out onto the landing of the steps which led down to the tarmac, he had to shield his eyes from the bright sunlight. The air was so clear he could see for miles as he surveyed the scene before him. Sydney airport. At last. He didn't think they were ever going to get here.

Packing up seemed to take weeks even before they'd left the house. The flight from San Francisco to L.A. hadn't taken long, but once they landed in L.A. it took another hour to find the right departure gate for the flight to Sydney. Then there was a 2-hour delay because of a "technical adjustment." The flight seemed to go on forever, but at least it was broken by a short stop-over in Honolulu.

As he stood there, taking it all in, he was filled with an elation he had never felt before. The start of their Big Adventure! *Mum would have loved this,* he thought, as he descended the steps in front of his father. She would also have said: 'Seize the day, Tom. Enjoy every moment. You may never pass this way again.'

As they made their way to the luggage carousel and stood waiting for their suitcases, Tom looked around at the milling crowd and then glanced up at his father. 'This airport is a bit bigger than I thought it'd be. I love how they talk,' he said, grinning at his father. Jim looked down and winked at him. 'Wait until you see where we're going to live.'

Their bags were among the first ones to come off the plane, and once they were sure they had the right suitcases, they made their way to the taxi rank outside the terminal, where a line of cabs was waiting.

The driver of the first cab in the line hurried around the cab to where Jim was picking up the largest suitcases. 'Here, I'll put those bags in the boot for you, mate,' he said, taking the suitcase from Jim.

'What did he say?' asked Tom quizzically.

'He means the trunk, but they call it the boot here,' replied Jim.

'Weird! Anything else I should know?' laughed Tom. 'Oh, you'll catch on soon enough,' said Jim as they climbed into the back seat of the cab.

'Double Bay, thanks driver,' said Jim as the taxi edged into the traffic.

'Been here before?' asked the cabbie, glancing in the rear-view mirror at them.

'I've been here a few times, but this is a first for my son. We'll be living here for the next year or two.'

'Well, you're in for a treat,' the cabbie replied, turning and looking in Tom's direction. 'You're only a stone's throw away from Bondi, the best beach in the world.' He said, proudly. 'It's only a few kilometres from where I'll drop you.'

'What did he say?' whispered Tom, turning to his father.

'He means we're going to be close to Bondi Beach. It's a beautiful beach, even if the size of it is a bit overwhelming at first.'

Tom continued to stare out the window of the cab, amazed and delighted at everything he saw—the streets were narrower than they were back home and there were no freeways, which probably explained why there was much less heavy traffic. The buildings were so different from each other. Some seemed quite old, while others looked brand new with lots of glass and colourful signage. And where were all the black people? Everyone they passed on the sidewalks or in parks seemed so "Australian." And there were buses everywhere! It didn't seem as glitzy as San Francisco; it felt smaller and more comfortable. Tom relaxed as he began to enjoy this cab ride. This city of

Sydney felt friendly and welcoming, more like a country town back home.

'I know Double Bay is on this side of the harbour, but would it be possible to cross the Harbour Bridge then come back so Tom here can see the harbour from the bridge?' Jim enquired of the driver.

'No worries,' replied the driver, delighted to be their tour guide for the next half hour.

The number of cars on the road increased as they approached the city. Pedestrians scuttled out of the way as traffic lights turned green and cars and trucks picked up speed. They drove in a complete circle through a tunnel before emerging into the sunshine once again as they approached the Harbour Bridge. *This is so exciting,* thought Tom, *if the kids from school could see me now! Although, it's a bit strange how they drive on the left side of the road. Feels dangerous.*

And onto the Sydney Harbour Bridge. 'You could not have picked a better day to see the harbour,' said the cabbie., 'But it looks good in the rain too.' *Sure is different than the Golden Gate back home,* thought Tom.

Tom was spellbound. It didn't matter where you looked; the harbour dominated. The blue water sparkled in the sunlight and sailboats and ferries dodged each other as they made white ribbons of wake in the blue water. His view was suddenly interrupted as a train sped past in the opposite direction. So much happening at once, so much to see, much busier than San Francisco Bay.

'On the left, which is the western side of the Bridge,' said the cabbie, slipping into his Tourist Guide persona, 'the Harbour eventually becomes the Parramatta River. On our right, the Harbour flows out into the Pacific Ocean between North and South Head, about fifteen K's from here.'

'They use kilometres here, instead of miles,' Tom's dad whispered in Tom's direction. 'That's what he means by K's.'

'Oh no, now I've got to learn about kilometres as well as all the other weird words and their meanings. I thought I'd pick up here where I left off back in California. I didn't realise it would be a whole new learning curve.'

'Aw, mate, you'll catch on in no time,' laughed the cabbie.

Tom relaxed back into the cab seat and consciously opened his mind and his heart to this wonderful new adventure which awaited him. Even though it had been a long flight and he was physically tired, he was aware of a feeling of excitement as the adrenalin flowed and he was carried along in the pleasure of the moment.

Once on the northern side of the harbour, the cabbie made a right-hand turn, and then another, and they found themselves back on the Bridge, heading south.

The Harbour looked even bigger and more spectacular from this side of the Bridge and Tom drank it all in with relish. *I'm going to be living here*, he thought to himself gleefully. *Tom Watson, how did you get so lucky?*

'Ah, you wouldn't be dead for quids on a day like today, would ya?' smiled the cabbie. 'God's own country.'

Tom glanced over at his father and they both stifled a laugh.

Fifteen minutes later, they pulled up in front of a small, white cottage nestled between two bigger and more imposing mansions on a pretty tree-lined street in Double Bay.

'This is it. Your new home away from home. I hope it's everything you want it to be,' said the cabbie. He walked around to the back of the cab, retrieved their suitcases and Tom's guitar case from the boot, and placed them on the footpath.

'Can I put this on a credit card?' asked Jim as he dug a card out of his wallet.

'No problem, mate,' the cabbie replied as he swiped the plastic card through the small machine. 'Sign here.'

'Would you have a pen I could use? I think I left mine on the plane,' said Jim as he felt his pockets.

'Sure, Mate. Here, use my biro.'

At which point Tom dissolved into laughter as he picked up a suitcase in one hand and his guitar case in the other, pushed open the front gate, and walked up the path to the front door.

'A Biro!!! Must remember that one. That's the best yet.'

www.ingramcontent.com/pod-product-compliance
Lightning Source LLC
Chambersburg PA
CBHW022052290426
44109CB00014B/1073